# Nick Drake | The complete guide to his music

Peter Hogan

**OMNIBUS PRESS**

London/New York/Paris/Sydney/Copenhagen/Berlin/Madrid/Tokyo

**Exclusive Distributors**
Music Sales Limited,
14/15 Berners Street,
London, W1T 3LJ.

Music Sales Corporation,
257 Park Avenue South,
New York, NY 10010, USA.

Macmillan Distribution Services,
53 Park West Drive,
Derrimut, Vic 3030,
Australia.

Every effort has been made to trace the copyright holders of the
photographs in this book but one or two were unreachable. We would be
grateful if the photographers concerned would contact us.

Typeset by Phoenix Photosetting, Chatham, Kent
Printed by Gutenberg Press Ltd, Malta

A catalogue record for this book is available from the British Library.

Visit Omnibus Press on the web at www.omnibuspress.com

# Contents

# Introduction

## I: Fame Is But A Fruit Tree

Nick Drake made just three albums before his death at the age of 26 in 1974. At that point, his total record sales were a mere 20,000. In all probability, even fewer people than that ever saw him play live. He only ever gave one press interview. There is no film footage of him after his childhood, and comparatively few photographs; these show a tall, elegant young man with a slight stoop and elfin good looks.

During his lifetime, most people discovered Nick Drake either by total accident, as I did (through hearing 'Time Has Told Me' on the 1969 Island sampler *Nice Enough To Eat*), or else by word of mouth recommendation. As the decades passed, that word of mouth accelerated and snowballed to the point that snatches of Nick's music now seem to follow you wherever you go; as his one-time collaborator John Cale put it recently, "every time I go to Starbucks I hear it". His reputation had been enhanced by three posthumous collections of unreleased material, and also by as many 'best of' compilations. Over the last ten years or so Nick's music has appeared on the soundtracks of at least one TV commercial and at least five movies. He's been the subject of two substantial biographies (by Patrick Humphries and Trevor

Dann) and a number of TV and radio documentaries; there's talk of an official biography in the works, and even the possibility of a film version of his life. Numerous websites and message boards are devoted to exhaustively analysing his life and music, and both his grave in Tanworth-in-Arden and his old family home Far Leys nearby, have become sites of pilgrimage for a steady trickle of devoted fans.

Since Nick's death his work has been praised by (among others) Elton John, Peter Buck, Robyn Hitchcock, Tom Verlaine, Paul Weller, the Dream Academy's Nick Laird-Clowes, The The's Matt Johnson, Clive Gregson, Elvis Costello, the Red Hot Chili Peppers, Kate Bush, Mark Eitzel, Belle & Sebastian, the Cardigans, the Black Crowes, Stephen Duffy and Everything But The Girl's Ben Watt. Hollywood icons Brad Pitt and Jennifer Aniston had Nick's music played at their wedding (Pitt went on to narrate a BBC radio documentary about the singer, and was rumoured to have even considered playing him in a biopic). Both Joe Boyd and Robert Kirby have been sought out by numerous other artists keen to work with them after hearing their work with Nick. He's also inspired a number of songs by other artists, most of whom knew him personally: Robin Frederick's 'Sandy Grey' (recorded by John Martyn on *London Conversation*), John Martyn's 'Solid Air', Richard Thompson's 'The Poor Boy Is Taken Away', Ashley Hutchings' 'Given Time' and Robyn Hitchcock's 'I Saw Nick Drake'.

Today, Nick's music has reached an incredibly broad audience, of all ages and tribes. So what's at the heart of his appeal? His death is certainly a part of it, if only because he's frozen forever in youth; his good looks will never be ravaged by age, his music will never decline. With the distance of time, Nick's essential shyness has become transformed into enigmatic charisma, his sad fate now an integral extension of his romantic music. But ultimately, it's the music that counts.

During the late sixties Nick was just one of many English singer-songwriters spinning out of the folk clubs – a group that included Ralph McTell, John Martyn, Al Stewart, Roy Harper and many others – and it was inevitable that he'd be bracketed alongside them; but time has proved that Nick was far more talented than any of his contemporaries. He was possessed of a pure, English singing voice – something that was still rare (if not unique) at the time – with a vocal style that was all his own. Instrumentally, as Joe Boyd has pointed out, Nick's guitar playing seems at first hearing to be quite straightforward and simple; it's only when you pay close attention that you realise how subtle and involved it really is. Nick employed open guitar tunings that were incredibly complex; numerous guitarists have since been completely baffled as to exactly how Nick did what he did, the tunings being impossible to figure out from simply listening to records. In addition, Nick's picking style came from the fact that he was steeped in 12-bar blues … and there are other influences audible as well that are not usually found in folk music, such as modern jazz and baroque classical music (Nick was particularly fond of Delius and Chopin). He could play a number of instruments, could read and write music, and had very broad musical tastes. Lyrically, his songs are noticeably more literate and intelligent than those of most songwriters of his time, perhaps because none of them had studied literature at Cambridge, as Nick had done.

His music has frequently been called 'timeless', and it's often commented that it could have been recorded yesterday. This may be because it wasn't popular in its own time, and thus has no associations with that era. Secondly, although much of the ground that Nick covered was highly personal, it remained free of the confessional self-indulgence common to many other singer-songwriters of his time. Finally, at least some of the time Nick was attempting to convey – without the clichés of the sixties – a sense of wonder and a sense of magic; much of his early work concerns nature, and man's place in it, while his later songs concern how city life affects us, how it can distance us from the things that really matter. These are themes that are not confined to any era in particular; one might almost call them eternal truths.

# II: Know

Nick Drake's work is inevitably overshadowed by the illness of his later years, and the nature of his death. Despite the official verdict of suicide, it's equally possible that the overdose of antidepressants that killed him was simply taken accidentally. Either way, his death remains a tragedy – and one that's easy to romanticise. The central mysteries of Nick's life and death will never be solved, but it's both inevitable and understandable that many of his fans have chosen to project their own pet theories and fantasies upon his story.

Given that Nick barely spoke to his friends or family – let alone the press – about his work or his life, we're left with only his songs as a source for possibly understanding what he might have thought about the world. There are many who find Nick's music sad and/or depressing (though I am not one of them); these are perhaps the same people who – knowing that Nick had read both Camus and Sartre – conclude that his world view was an existentialist one. This is simply not true. Admittedly, much of Nick's later work deals with alienation and isolation, but even *Pink Moon* ends with the incredibly joyous and positive 'From The Morning' – and all of his early work displays a deep reverence for nature, and what might best be described as a form of optimistic pantheism. It comes as no surprise to learn that Nick was a firm believer in James Lovelock's Gaia theory, that all life on Earth is interconnected.

He was also known to have read some Buddhist texts, and the critic Ian MacDonald detected a definite Buddhist influence upon Nick's life and work, citing several references to reincarnation in his songs, his complete lack of interest in material possessions and his observed compassion for other people. Certainly, Nick referred more than once in his songs to "magic", and was definitely interested in the transcendent, in the world of the spirit – and this interest was one he held in common with most of the hippie generation. When *Time* magazine coined the phrase "God is dead" to comment on the decline of Christianity, Leonard Cohen swiftly responded: "God is alive, magic is afoot." The spiritual quest of the hippie era was not entirely shallow and superficial; at its core was something quite genuine, which stood right at the heart of the generation gap – which was not a question of age, but of fundamental world view. Those who had lived through the Great Depression and World War II understandably wanted nothing more than material prosperity, as a response to the chaos they had been forced to endure. But it was not enough for their children, who were also keenly aware that they were living in the Cold War shadow of imminent nuclear holocaust. The hippies sought spiritual answers to the fundamental questions of life, but those answers were not to be found in orthodox religion any more than in materialism. Drug-taking in the late Sixties was not simply a matter of escapist hedonism, but an honest – if misguided – attempt to explore the boundaries of consciousness; to force open the doors of perception, and see heaven in a wild flower. When drugs proved a dead end, many ventured down other avenues – and of course, many of these also led nowhere (Nick's friend Ross Grainger told Trevor Dann that he and Nick had often discussed "spirits, Stonehenge, ley lines and the little people"). But if some beliefs of the hippies were the ones would evolve into New Age twaddle, others were more worthy. From Eastern mysticism came the notions that everyone and everything are all a part of the same universal process, that every life has dignity and meaning, and that the motivating force that causes every star to shine and every human heart to pulse is nothing less than pure love. These beliefs resonate deeply within Nick's work, and are central to understanding it.

Ian MacDonald also believed that Nick employed his own 'poetic language', which relied heavily on nature symbolism and had its roots in his country upbringing; if you are able to read the symbols, Nick's words then take on a deeper meaning. This was to some extent confirmed by Robin Frederick, who has stated that 'Saturday' definitely referred to Nick's time in Aix. MacDonald thought that 'rain' stood for transformation, 'summer' for innocence, 'blue' for sights that invoke a Buddhist sense of compassion, 'Sunday' for disenchantment and the 'sun' for God's influence on Earth; the sea represented a moment of respite, or death before rebirth, while the moon stood for drugs and illusion, including the pull of materialistic desire.

MacDonald's excellent essay on Nick can be found in his book *The People's Music*. His theory may or may not be correct, but the idea of Nick employing a poetic language isn't too far-fetched, given that he was studying poetry. One major influence upon him is known to have been the mystical poet William Blake (Molly Drake said her son believed Blake to have been "the only good British poet"); Yeats was another influence (also mystical), as were the Romantic poets, who virtually deified nature. Nick's work is definitely romantic in the classical sense, with a spiritual/mystical core that concerns itself with the deeper meaning of existence – but unlike most of the hippie generation, Nick wasn't content with reducing this topic to simple slogans that could be worn as that year's accessories. As MacDonald puts it, his work was "too allusive – and not mundanely optimistic enough – to appeal to his contemporaries".

This would explain Nick's sense of failure far more than his lack of funds. If his anger at his lack of success was partly a side effect of the pills he was prescribed, it also partly sprang from genuine frustration; he felt he had something to say, and it just wasn't being heard. John Martyn once observed that Nick felt that the world "had not quite lived up to his expectations". His own sister has called him both "stubborn" and "a perfectionist"; she also thought he had "a skin too few". But even Buddhists can have bad days, and Nick undoubtedly had far more than his share.

## III: The Poor Boy is Taken Away

It's no secret that, Nick suffered from mental problems. Although some have speculated that he was an undiagnosed schizophrenic, this seems so extreme a verdict as to be improbable – someone, somewhere, would have spotted the signs sooner or later. What no one disputes is that Nick's key problem was one of depression, though some question whether it was actually clinical depression as we understand it today. Nick's friend Brian Wells, who later became a psychiatrist, thought that Nick had somehow got himself into an "existential state". It's been suggested by others that Nick's depression could have at least partly been caused by seasonal affective disorder. Whatever the truth, Nick's illness occurred long before psychotherapy became acceptable; at the time, even consulting a psychiatrist carried a terrible social stigma. Sadly, no one ever got to the heart of Nick's problems; as was typical in those days, he was prescribed some pills and then turned loose in the world. His friends might have helped, but none knew how, nor did Nick ever ask for aid. He was a creative artist, doing his own thing; to even ask about a person's personal life in those days would have been uncool, and the concept of intervention unthinkable.

Nick's depression was almost certainly fuelled by his introspective nature. John Martyn once called him "the most withdrawn person I've ever met." Linda Thompson, who dated Nick, observed that "he made monosyllabic seem quite chatty", and those who worked with him all said that he communicated far better musically than he did verbally. Nick had always been the first one to leave parties and other social events; some think that this was an affectation, that Nick was deliberately cultivating a romantic aura of mystery. But he had always been contemplative and reflective, and was given to seeking quiet and solitude from an early age. Still, it's clear that Nick's descent into depression was without doubt an arc of ever-increasing isolation: from being part of a group to playing solo; from a gregarious social life in Cambridge to a solitary existence in London; from working with other musicians, an arranger and a producer to recording with just one person in the control booth. Now, while a degree of solitude is almost essential to the creative life, and can be an enormously positive force for good, at the far edges of it lie the borders of madness. In Nick's later years, there are countless stories of him sitting in total silence, staring into nothingness.

How much of a part did drugs play in this decline? Nick certainly habitually smoked large quantities of hashish, and in his biography of Nick, *Darker Than The Deepest Sea*,

Trevor Dann cites several recent medical reports linking teenage cannabis use with the onset of psychosis and/or schizophrenia. However, these reports largely concern marijuana use, especially with regard to modern mutated strains of the drug such as skunk. The link between skunk and psychosis is well established but, according to some authorities, skunk is up to 25 times stronger than hashish, and effectively a completely different drug. That's not to say that cannabis didn't affect Nick's mental state adversely, merely that it's by no means certain; at the very least, it's true that it probably didn't help matters. For someone as introspective as Nick, chain-smoking hash in solitude certainly wasn't the healthiest of lifestyles – and it may well have mixed badly with the antidepressants he was taking.

Nick is also said to have expressed a curiosity about heroin but, although he almost certainly knew people who used it, there's no evidence that he ever took heroin himself. If he did, he never got hooked (again, someone would have noticed). On the other hand, he certainly did take magic mushrooms, and is thought to have tried LSD at least once, perhaps more than that. The dosages for acid trips in those days are said to have been approximately ten times stronger than in more recent times; everyone who survived that era knows of at least one person who took a trip and never really came back again. At the very least, acid tended to permanently change the way people viewed 'reality', and it's probably no accident that the word 'strange' occurs in a lot of Nick's Aix-era songs. LSD also tends to bring a person's problems into sharp relief, which is partly why it can be so horrific – and also why the drug was such a useful psychiatric tool, before its clinical use was banned. But once those problems have surfaced, they then have to be faced and dealt with, and this may have been a battle Nick fought for the rest of his days.

It should also be remembered that it was the antidepressant Tryptizol that actually killed him. The journalist Nick Kent – no stranger to drug use himself – was once prescribed Tryptizol as an aid to getting himself off heroin, and told Patrick Humphries that the pills were "horrible, horrible drugs", and that taking just two of the tablets had turned him into "a brain-dead zombie" for about 72 hours. Many of the symptoms Nick displayed in his final years were clearly side effects of these pills; far from helping, they may well have made him a lot worse.

Poor record sales and a sense of personal failure probably didn't help matters either, since his work was really all Nick had. But it's doubtful these were crucial factors in his depression; whatever was at the heart of Nick's problems was probably quite deep-rooted. Since his family upbringing seems to have been a happy one, let's consider another area of Nick's past: his single-sex education. For many, this experience throws up sexual inhibitions that can take years to recover from – and some people never do.

There are those who believe Nick was a repressed homosexual – or at the very least bisexual – but those who knew him at school and university saw no indication of it, and there seems to be no other evidence for it at all. He was certainly repressed, though, and cripplingly shy; for all that his music is so sensual, his love songs are usually those of an onlooker. Yet, as Robert Kirby told Patrick Humphries, "All women liked him. I remember all my girlfriends fancied him." There are many other accounts along these lines, but Nick apparently always seemed oblivious to this attention. Robin Frederick admits she was in love with Nick, but that they never actually had a relationship. Linda Peters (later Thompson) dated him and tried to seduce him, but without success; she also claims another female friend had a similar experience. Even Sophia Ryde – with whom Nick definitely seemed to want a relationship – stresses the 'friend' part of girlfriend when describing their romance. There are a few anecdotes that suggest otherwise, but one could still easily believe that Nick might well have died a virgin. His early unreleased song 'Blue Season' refers to "lovers and losers that fail in the night", and it may be that Nick experienced some disastrous emotional and/or sexual encounter long before he met Linda Peters, and avoided the possibility of another failure ever afterwards. 'Tragedy' is an overused word that has lost its power to touch us; say instead that – if Nick's isolation was truly that complete – this is something that is heartbreakingly, brutally sad.

## IV: Now We Rise

To dwell too much on the misery of Nick's later years is to lessen his triumph. He once told his father that he had music running through his head all the time. Fortunately, despite all the demons that plagued him, he was still able to share at least some of that music with the world – and it remains some of the most beautiful pop music ever made. This is Nick Drake's true legacy; the rest is merely legend.

# Acknowledgements

# Acknowledgements

My thanks to Patrick Humphries and Sue Parr, and to the late Ian MacDonald. I'm also indebted to the work of all the other writers who have chronicled Nick's life and career, notably Arthur Lubow, Nick Kent, Joe Boyd and Trevor Dann.

Thanks also to Chris Charlesworth at Omnibus, to Maureen Hughes once again, and most of the Unusual Suspects: Ellie, Quinn and Hal.

*Peter Hogan, London, 2008.*

# Prelude

# One of These Things First – The Early Years

Rodney Drake met Mary – known to all as Molly – Lloyd in Rangoon, Burma, where he was working as an executive in the teak trade. Molly was 18 at the time. Two years later Rodney proposed, and the couple married the following year. During World War II the Drakes were evacuated to India, and their first child, Gabrielle (who would later become a successful actress), was born in Lahore in 1944. After the war the family briefly returned to Rangoon, which is where Nicholas Rodney Drake was born on June 19, 1948.

The Drakes were a product of Empire, and decidedly upper middle class (Nick's spoken voice was much posher than many of his fans realise), but when Burma became independent the writing was on the wall for Rodney's career there; it was time to leave. The family returned to Britain in the early Fifties, when Nick was about four years old. In 1953, Rodney became managing director of the Wolseley Engineering Company in Birmingham, a position that would secure his financial prosperity for the rest of his life (by most people's standards, the Drakes were actually quite wealthy). The family settled in the nearby Warwickshire village of Tanworth-in-Arden, buying Far Leys House, where Rodney and Molly remained until long after Nick was dead ('Leys' is pronounced 'lees' – and nothing whatsoever to do with ley lines). By all accounts the Drakes were a very happy – and very close – family, and Gabrielle Drake has stated that she and her brother enjoyed "an idyllic childhood". Rodney and Molly were both fond of music, and in their youth both had tried their hand at songwriting (Rodney had even written a complete operetta); in 2007, two recordings of Molly playing the piano and singing her songs surfaced on the *Family Tree* album, and it's clear that she had at least some influence upon her son's musical style. Nick grew up surrounded by music, both classical and popular, and both he and his sister were first taught piano by Molly, and then took private lessons. According to Gabrielle, Nick wrote his first songs at the age of three or four, and the two of them performed duets inspired by the quasi-folk duo Nina and Frederick.

Having attended the local pre-preparatory school, Hurst House, from the age of five, Nick was sent away to board at Eagle House preparatory school just before his ninth birthday; when he was 13, he transferred to the Wiltshire public school Marlborough College, which both his father and grandfather before him had attended. Both schools were for boys only. At Eagle House Nick played rugby, acted in the school play, sang in the school choir; at Marlborough he became an extremely good runner. His school friends recall him as being popular, clever and funny; in school photographs he looks relaxed and happy (a startling contrast with his later image). In his final year at Marlborough he was captain of his house.

He liked art, "Goya, and modern art in particular", and discovered French literature (notably Balzac, Sartre and

Camus); like any other teenager of the era he also discovered rock 'n' roll, cigarettes and beer. He now played clarinet and alto saxophone as well as piano, and music occupied much of his time. He played in Marlborough's military cadet band, and also joined a school rock group named The Perfumed Gardeners, which sometimes included as many as eight people, including a trombone player. The group's name was derived from *The Perfumed Garden*, a 16th century classic of erotic literature translated by the Victorian explorer Sir Richard Burton, which had only recently been published in Britain for the first time, and which had made quite an impact (in 1967 the DJ John Peel also named his first British radio show after the book). The Perfumed Gardeners' music was blues-based rock, the Yardbirds and Rolling Stones being their major influences. Nick acted as the band's music director, arranging most of the material; he was also (reluctantly) their vocalist, since he was the only one who could actually sing. A slightly younger Marlborough pupil named Chris Davison desperately wanted to join the band but was turned down; he would later find fame under the name Chris De Burgh. In his final years at school Nick bought himself an acoustic guitar for £13 (a very large amount of money at the time) and began teaching himself to play (his Marlborough friend David Wright taught him his first chords). Within two years, he'd become one of the most dazzlingly inventive and original guitarists of all time. Although he played standing up on rare occasions, he was nearly always seated to play.

A brief summary of Nick's musical influences during his Marlborough days would include John Coltrane, Graham Bond, Zoot Money, Miles Davis, Charlie Parker, John Hammond, Jimmy Smith, Django Reinhardt, the Supremes, Booker T & the MGs, Astrud Gilberto & Stan

Getz, Odetta, Bob Dylan, Mose Allison, Josh White, Brownie McGhee, Muddy Waters and Howlin' Wolf. While still at school Nick made several excursions to London to see bands playing live at clubs such as the Marquee and the Flamingo, including Zoot Money, Georgie Fame, Chris Farlowe and the Spencer Davis Group.

In the summer of 1965 Nick flunked his A-level exams, and was forced to stay on at Marlborough for an extra year to re-take them. In July 1966 Nick acquired four A-levels, but his grades (apart from in English) were poor. So, that autumn he spent an extra term at the cramming college Birmingham Tutorial School before taking the Oxford and Cambridge scholarship exam. Having passed, he was offered a place to read English at Fitzwilliam College, Cambridge, commencing in the autumn of 1967.

Since part of his course would require the ability to translate from French into English, Nick needed to improve his proficiency in the language, so his parents enrolled him in a six-month-long course at the Université de Aix-en-Provence in France. This was fine with Nick, who liked the country, and had spent the previous two summers there with schoolfriends (David Wright and Jeremy Mason respectively).

In February 1967 Nick travelled to Aix with friends Simon Crocker and Jeremy Mason, who were also taking the same course; while there the trio became friends with another Englishman, Roddy Llewellyn, later to achieve tabloid notoriety as Princess Margaret's near-constant companion. In Aix Nick discovered Baudelaire and Rimbaud; but he was by this point far more interested in music than in literature. He practised the guitar for hours on end, experimenting with different tunings; he wrote his very first songs, did a little busking on the streets of Aix and St Tropez and made his first demo tape. Two albums he discovered during this period that both had a big influence on his evolving guitar style were Donovan's *Mellow Yellow* and Phil Ochs' *Changes*. In Aix he also became friends with an American girl named Robin Frederick. She was a 19-year-old singer-songwriter who sang both cover versions and her own original songs (one of which Nick would later record), and it's clear that she also had a musical influence on him (and quite possibly an emotional one as well). It's possible that Nick also took LSD while in Aix, and he had certainly already discovered hashish by then.

In Aix Nick also fell in with another crowd of English friends – richer and wilder, and decidedly upper class. In March 1967 Nick and several of these other friends travelled to Morocco, where they stayed for a month, driving around fairly aimlessly and smoking a good deal of hash. En route they encountered the holidaying Mick Jagger and Keith Richards (plus retinue) in a restaurant, where Nick's friends bullied him into playing some Dylan and Donovan songs to impress the rock stars. It evidently worked, as Nick and his friends were invited to join the Stones for lunch.

After returning home, Nick spent 1967's Summer of Love in London, staying with Gabrielle at her flat in Battersea and mixing with her high-society friends (and others he'd met in France), some of whom had rock music connections. Much of his time was spent smoking hash with friends such as photographer Julian Lloyd (whose photo of Nick would grace the cover of the compilation album *Way To Blue*) and his girlfriend Victoria Ormsby-Gore. Through them Nick met Sophia Ryde, who was at that time dating someone else but with whom he would eventually forge a friendship that was to be of lasting significance.

That autumn he departed for Cambridge, where his music would become much more than just a hobby.

# Five Leaves Left

*Island ILPS 9105 (LP); IMCD 8 (CD); released September 1969.*
*Produced by Joe Boyd. All compositions by Nick Drake.*

In October 1967 Nick Drake entered Fitzwilliam College, Cambridge, to read English Literature. He bought himself a motorbike, auditioned (unsuccessfully) for the Cambridge Footlights revue and enjoyed punting and parties. Fitzwilliam was a modern, red-brick complex some distance away from the other university colleges, then a single-sex institution jointly dominated by the sciences and sport. Nick reportedly hated the brutal modernity of the place, and its rowdy sports-loving students. Although a resident of Fitzwilliam for his first year, Nick spent much of his time visiting friends at the other colleges, and frequently played his songs to entertain whoever was around.

Favourite items in Nick's record collection during his Cambridge days included Tim Buckley, Randy Newman's first album, The Byrds, Leonard Cohen, Tim Hardin, Love's *Forever Changes*, Van Morrison's *Astral Weeks*, Laura Nyro, Steve Miller's *Sailor* and Jimmy Webb's work with The Fifth Dimension. Inevitably, his guitar style was heavily influenced by the leading folk guitarists of the day, notably Bert Jansch, John Renbourn, Davey Graham and John

Martyn; the influence of Joni Mitchell is also detectable. Nick was also steeped in old blues, and was known to impress listeners during blues jams at Cambridge. He still experimented with his playing for hours on end, trying out different tunings; it's said that he often wrote his songs in a patchwork manner, perfecting them one guitar phrase at a time. Lyrically, he may well have been influenced by the French Symbolist poetry he was studying.

His Cambridge contemporaries recall him as being pleasant, shy, sensitive, quiet, detached and self-conscious, his speech somewhat hesitant; even so he possessed, as Robert Kirby told Patrick Humphries, "this incredible presence". His impact was partly physical – at 6′ 3″ he was imposingly tall (although thin with it), but subject to what Joe Boyd called an "apologetic stoop"; he walked with what has been described as a loping gait. Despite being so large, he's often spoken of as being fragile and elegant, although Joe Boyd has also described Nick's hands and fingers as being "very large, and incredibly strong". He wore his hair long but was clean-shaven, and was stylishly dressed (for the time) in a black velvet jacket, black cord jeans and Cuban-heeled boots. But some maintain that Nick never cared about his appearance, and that even in his university days his clothes were often stained with cigarette ash, his shoes worn out and his shirts frayed. He frequently wore the same clothes for days on end. His fingers were also heavily stained by nicotine, and according to Joe Boyd at their first meeting Nick's nails were also "caked with grime".

Nick supplemented his student grant by selling psychedelic posters (imported from California, bought by Nick in London) to his fellow students. Academically, he was far from an ideal student, and did the absolute minimum of coursework. One reason for this was that his musical career was already in motion. In late 1967, Nick approached Chris

Blackwell at Island Records, and played him a demo tape of his songs. Blackwell was intrigued, but felt that Island didn't really know how to market solo singers (although they'd already signed John Martyn). Blackwell offered Nick some vague encouragement, and told him to get in touch again after a few months. Then, a week or so before Christmas 1967 (and just two months after arriving at Cambridge), Nick played his first professional solo gig, as one of the support acts to Country Joe & the Fish at the Roundhouse in London. No one knows exactly how Nick ended up on the bill, but presumably he must have actively put himself forward for the gig. Fairport Convention also played the Roundhouse that night, and Fairport's Ashley Hutchings stayed on after his band's set; at around three in the morning, he caught Nick's performance. Struck by Nick's good looks, his musical style and "magnetic" presence, Hutchings afterwards told Nick that he should contact his own manager, Joe Boyd; he also passed on Nick's phone number to Boyd, suggesting he investigate this intriguing new singer. Nick duly met up with Boyd but said very little, simply handing over a demo tape that he'd recorded at home in Tanworth over the Christmas break.

Joe Boyd was an American with impeccable credentials in the London music scene. Born in 1942, he'd toured the States with blues acts and helped produce the Newport Folk Festival in 1965, the year that Dylan went electric. At the end of that year Boyd moved to England, to run the London office of the American record label Elektra. Although the job didn't last, Boyd decided to stay on in the city, and in 1966 he co-founded UFO, the hippest club of the hippie era, which kick-started the careers of the Soft Machine and Pink Floyd (among many others). He then produced the Floyd's debut single, 'Arnold Layne', but their label, EMI, didn't want him to produce their album.

Instead, at the end of 1966 Boyd set up his own company, Witchseason (named after the Donovan song 'Season Of The Witch'), to act as an umbrella for all the areas of music in which he was involved: artist management, concert promotion and record production; music publishing was handled by Witchseason's sister company, Warlock (a name that both The Incredible String Band and Nick Drake found disquieting. Nick had attended several séances while in Aix, and one of them had spooked him badly, so he may well have been wary of anything that sounded even vaguely supernatural). At this point Boyd had already discovered Fairport Convention, The Incredible String Band and John & Beverley Martyn, and was on the verge of signing a deal whereby all Witchseason recordings would be released through Island Records.

"The first time I heard the songs I immediately knew I wanted to make a record with him," Boyd later said of the demo tape that Drake had left with him, which included versions of 'I Was Made To Love Magic', 'The Thoughts Of Mary Jane' and 'Time Has Told Me'. Boyd knew at once that the quality of the material was head and shoulders above every other demo he was receiving in those days, and "mysteriously original". He later commented that Nick's "guitar technique was so clean it took a while to realise how complex it was."

At their next meeting, Nick played Boyd all of his other songs. The producer was stunned by the faultless standard of Nick's playing (Molly Drake later observed that even as a child Nick was "an absolute perfectionist"), as well as its stylistic range. "After finishing one song, he would retune the guitar and proceed to play something equally complex in a totally different chord shape," Boyd recalled in his autobiography, *White Bicycles*. This was one of the cornerstones of Nick's musical approach, and one that dazzled his listeners;

unfortunately, it would also cause him immense problems during live performance. Boyd and Drake also discussed how those songs should be arranged on record, and agreed that strings should play a major part (Boyd recalls enthusing over John Simon's production of the first Leonard Cohen album).

It took many more discussions before recording sessions for what would become the *Five Leaves Left* album began in October 1968 (and continued sporadically for much of the next year). The main venue was Sound Techniques studio, located in a former dairy in London's Chelsea, just off the King's Road. The resident engineer here was John Wood, who was to become one of the key figures in Nick's life; he engineered his first two albums and produced the third. Nick trusted him utterly, and Wood both liked and was extremely protective of Nick ("John Wood loved Nick," Joe Boyd later recalled). The reasons for the lengthy time span of the recordings were twofold. Firstly, Nick was still officially studying at Cambridge, and a lengthy absence from there would not have gone down well with either his tutor or his parents; secondly, recording the album a couple of songs at a time allowed a pause for reflection, the better to build a coherent whole. Boyd always relished the opportunity to add ingredients and generally experiment. But the first sessions at Sound Techniques didn't go well, with Nick seemingly suffering slightly from nerves; around this time Nick was beginning his second year at Cambridge, and finally moved out of halls. He lived briefly in a small room in Carlyle Road, but didn't get on with the old-fashioned landlady there and quickly moved again, this time to Chesterton Road. Nick doesn't seem to have spent much of his spare time there, and was often to be found at Robert Kirby's room in Green Street.

The next recording sessions took place at Morgan Studios in early 1969. Having searched for a suitable orchestral arranger, Boyd recruited Richard Hewson, who had worked with The Beatles on 'The Long And Winding Road' and on Mary Hopkin's 'Those Were The Days', as well as arranging James Taylor's eponymous debut album. At the first session Boyd realised that Hewson's mainstream arrangements didn't fit and were "distracting from the songs rather than adding to them". Evidently relieved, Nick recommended that they should work instead with his fellow Cambridge student, Robert Kirby

Kirby, who was on a music scholarship at Caius College, had met Nick during his first week at Cambridge, when both of them had unsuccessfully auditioned for the Footlights revue (the panel of judges included Clive James, and possibly also Germaine Greer). The two quickly became friends, and a musical collaboration of some kind seemed inevitable. Kirby was also a member of a close-harmony singing group, The Gentle Power Of Song, who had recorded several singles and an album for Polydor. Knowing this, Nick asked Kirby to come up with orchestral arrangements for some of his songs, and – since Nick had been lending him records to listen to, including The Fifth Dimension's *Magic Garden* and the first Randy Newman album – Kirby had at least some idea of what Nick had in mind. Nick also explained what he wanted in terms of instrumentation, but because his playing used what Kirby considered "strange tunings" that were "very complicated" and completely unlike conventional guitar tunings, Kirby made Nick play through his songs while noting down exactly how each chord and bar was played. It was a painstaking process, to put it mildly, but it would pay off. They also recorded a tape of Nick playing his songs in Kirby's room.

The first results of their partnership surfaced shortly before Easter 1968, when Nick played a concert at the Bateman Room of Gonville & Caius College Cambridge, in front of an audience of approximately 60 people. The purpose was to test-drive Kirby's arrangements, and the musicians present included a string quartet, two flautists, a double-bass player and a French horn player. Unfortunately, there had been no time for any rehearsal, and the musicians had only been given the sheet music shortly before going on stage; the results were thus somewhat chaotic. The concert was recorded by Peter Rice, who later also recorded Nick playing more songs solo (at Nick's request), and added these to the Bateman tape; Nick is known to have used this as a demo tape, possibly simply to convince Boyd that Kirby was worth talking to. It's also possible that Nick was still keeping his options open and was talking to other people in the music business; at this point he had yet to sign a contract with Boyd. It's also worth noting that Nick seemingly had no problems playing in front of an audience in his Cambridge days; in addition to impromptu performances in front of groups of friends and other students, he also played at folk clubs, including several appearances at an old Cambridge pub called The Bun Shop.

At some point during summer 1968, Nick signed a contract with Joe Boyd, which stipulated that the latter was to act as his manager, agent, song publisher and record producer – presumably Boyd's standard contract. As such, Boyd was effectively both Nick's mentor and his patron (once the contract was signed, Nick began to receive a stipend of £10 per week); Boyd's evident talent and contacts hopefully more than compensated for the downside (this being that Nick had no one else on hand to advise him, either creatively or financially). Since Nick was still under 21 at the time (which was then the age of majority), his parents' signature was required on the contract. Somehow, he persuaded them.

Back to 1969, and Nick's attempt to interest Boyd in using Robert Kirby's arrangements. The producer agreed to meet with Kirby, and was encouraged enough by seeing the evident chemistry between him and Nick to give the young arranger a try, despite not actually having heard any of Kirby's work. Sessions resumed at Sound Techniques with the Kirby-arranged tracks 'Way To Blue', 'Day Is Done', 'The Thoughts Of Mary Jane' and 'Fruit Tree'. These were recorded in one three-hour session, during which Nick played and sang live with the string quartet and bass; there were no overdubs. Both Boyd and John Wood were incredibly relieved when they heard the standard of Kirby's arrangements and Nick's performance.

Robert Kirby had struggled to come up with an arrangement for 'River Man' that fitted Nick's aspirations for the song, and had finally admitted defeat. Instead, Boyd brought in veteran arranger and session man Harry Robinson, who had once been a member of Lord Rockingham's Eleven and had also scored the soundtrack music for numerous Hammer horror movies. Nick had wanted the arrangement to be reminiscent of Delius, and had very specific ideas about how the string passages should be phrased, which he discussed with Robinson at length before the latter commenced work. For the arrangements of 'Time Has Told Me' and 'Man In A Shed', Boyd brought in pianist Paul Harris, who had been the musical director of John and Beverley Martyn's *Stormbringer* album.

Also on board for *Five Leaves Left* were Fairport Convention's guitarist Richard Thompson; Danny Thompson from Pentangle (who had also recorded with John Martyn and The Incredible String Band) on bass; Clare Lowther (who had also worked with the Strawbs and played on the first Fairport Convention album) on cello; Rocki Dzidzornu from Ghana on congas; and Tristan Fry on drums and vibraphone. Fry was a percussionist with the London Symphony Orchestra who played on sessions for a truly diverse range of artists, including Danny Kaye, Duke Ellington, The Beatles (on *Sgt Pepper*), Frank Sinatra, David Essex and Elton John; in the late Seventies he became a member of the progressive 'supergroup' Sky (which also included classical guitarist John Williams and bassist Herbie Flowers).

In June 1969, shortly after the album sessions concluded, Nick played two gigs in Cambridge accompanied by Robert Kirby and a mini-orchestra. The first of these took place in the library of Caius College, as part of their line-up for that year's May Ball, in front of an audience of 30–50. Accounts of this concert vary greatly, and it's possible that it's been confused with the Bateman concert the year before. It supposedly featured Kirby conducting a small string and woodwind section (including flautist/saxophonist Iain Cameron), with Colin Fleetcroft on string bass. Nick performed several songs unaccompanied in addition to the four that Kirby had arranged for, and linking the songs were instrumental passages from Albinoni's *Adagio* and Mozart's *Trumpet Concerto*. The female string section wore black evening gowns with white feather boas. The second gig took place at Cambridge's Pitt Club, as part of the 21st birthday celebrations for Brian Wells' girlfriend Marian, and also featured the string section.

The release of *Five Leaves Left* was delayed for several months by production problems. When it finally came out, it appeared in a stylish green-and-white sleeve that featured moody portraits of Nick by the photographer Keith Morris. The album title was a phrase printed on slips of paper inserted into packets of Rizla cigarette rolling papers that warned the user they were about to run out, ie that it was now time to go and buy another packet. It was thus a knowing in-joke for anyone who smoked cannabis. Patrick Humphries has suggested the possibility that the title may also refer to O. Henry's intimations-of-mortality short story *The Last Leaf*, which Nick could conceivably have stumbled across in his studies. Humphries also points out the eerie coincidence that the time period between the album's release and Nick's death is almost exactly five years.

There are many who think of *Five Leaves Left* as a sad record. It's certainly wistfully romantic, with an idealised view of love – as one might expect from a 20-year-old English student. But it would be unfair to call it adolescent, as some critics have done, since many of the songs here display a remarkable maturity – and as a debut, it's pretty remarkable. When released, the album received much acclaim from other musicians, although many of Nick's Cambridge contemporaries who had heard him play solo thought the string arrangements actually weakened his songs. As for the critics, *Five Leaves Left* was ignored by the underground press, the *NME* compared Nick unfavourably to Peter Sarstedt (an artist remembered today only for his mawkish hit 'Where Do You Go To My Lovely?'), while *Melody Maker* merely conceded the album was "interesting" (faint praise, if ever there was any).

Island Records had run no advertising campaign for the record at all; no singles were released from it (nor would there be from either of Nick's next two albums) and – apart from the occasional plug by John Peel – there was hardly any radio play. It was a desperate state of affairs, but Island knew exactly what should be done to improve matters: they wanted Nick to tour.

## TIME HAS TOLD ME

*Nick Drake, vocal and acoustic guitar; Paul Harris, piano;*
*Richard Thompson, electric guitar; Danny Thompson, bass.*

Possibly written in Aix-en-Provence in early 1967. The song seems to be looking back with regret, realising only after the event the true importance of a relationship – yet there's also acceptance of the status quo, and the confidence that things will come right in the end. Yet it's slightly ominous that – in what is effectively his musical debut – Nick admits to having a "troubled mind"; the "troubled cure" phrase would later inspire Robert Smith to name his band The Cure. "A soul with no footprint" would seem to indicate innocence, as would the "rose with no thorn". This latter image would seem to have been taken from Leonard McNally's 18th-century ballad 'Sweet Lass Of Richmond Hill' (set to music by James Hook and inspired by McNally's fiancé Miss Janson, who did indeed live on Richmond Hill). Musically, the song is practically a waltz, with Nick's delicate picking blending well with Danny Thompson's rumbling bass and Richard Thompson's tasteful guitar fills (the two Thompsons are not related). In November 1969 the track was included on the Island Records sampler *Nice Enough To Eat*. The song was also covered by Cassell Webb on her 1989 album *Songs Of A Stranger*.

## RIVER MAN

*Nick Drake, vocal and acoustic guitar; Harry Robinson, string arrangement.*

Recorded live with the orchestra, while Harry Robinson conducted. Ian MacDonald called this "one of the sky-high classics of post-war English popular music". It's also a strange blend of jazz and classical influences (some see an influence of Ravel here, others see Delius) in 5/4 time. The inspiration for the song may have come from two books that were cult novels at the time. The first is Herman Hesse's *Siddhartha*, where the protagonist spurns the aid of the Buddha only to receive enlightenment from an old ferryman (and his river). The second book is David Lindsay's 1920 science-fantasy epic *A Voyage To Arcturus*, a spiritual allegory comparable to a latter-day *Pilgrim's Progress*. During his travels across an alien world, the book's protagonist, Maskull, encounters a river that literally generates life before his eyes (like Nick, Lindsay is also thought to have been influenced by both William Blake and Buddhism). Of course, Nick could also be referring to Charon, the ferryman of the dead in Greek myth, but that would make the whole song much darker.

There may also be a more prosaic explanation, in that during the brief period when Nick was living in Cambridge's Carlyle Road he would have had to cross a short bridge every day in order to reach Jesus Green and the rest of the university. Regardless, while at Cambridge the river would still have been a key part of Nick's world; "all night shows in summertime" would seem to refer to the Cambridge May Balls (although shows at underground clubs such as UFO and Middle Earth also frequently lasted all night). Ian MacDonald thought the river definitely referred to the material world; the song's passage through the seasons (looking forward from autumn to the following summer) evokes not only the cyclic nature of the solar year, but also the Buddhist concept of the Wheel of Life (and the last line of the song undoubtedly refers to reincarnation). If this reading is true, then "Betty" has to choose between the material world and something higher (some think the inspiration for her name was the character Betty Foy in Wordsworth's poem *The Idiot Boy*, which Nick is known to have studied; MacDonald thought the name was a play on 'bet', ie the character is being called upon to take a chance). The song originally had an extra verse (quoted on the original album sleeve) which was not recorded in this version. Stephen 'Tintin' Duffy later named his band The Lilac Time after a line in the lyric. The phrase is also the title of two musical works that Nick may well have been familiar with through his parents: a 1910 song by Ernest Chausson and Maurice Bouchor, and a 1921 musical comedy by Wilner and Reichert (based upon music by Franz Schubert). 'River Man' has also been covered by Norma Waterson.

## THREE HOURS

*Nick Drake, vocal and acoustic guitar; Danny Thompson, bass; Rocki Dzidzornu, congas.*

"Jeremy" is Nick's Marlborough schoolmate Jeremy Mason, who'd also gone to Aix with him. Nick admitted to Mason that the song was about him, but wouldn't explain any more than that. Mason was baffled, but thought Nick might have been criticising him for his womanising – and since "Jacomo" is probably meant to imply Casanova, he could well be right. The master/slave line here certainly sounds as if it's intended to have a sexual meaning, despite Trevor Dann's suggestion that it may instead refer to themes within Hegelian philosophy. "Hoping to keep the sun from his eyes" implies that Jeremy is avoiding higher concerns and is somewhat shallow. As with 'River Man', this song originally had an extra verse (again quoted on the original album sleeve). Three hours would seem to refer to the journey time from Marlborough to London, and the song has a sense of urgency, its rhythm evoking that of a train. The song was wrongly credited as 'Sundown' on the original album sleeve.

## WAY TO BLUE

*Nick Drake, vocal; Robert Kirby, string arrangement.*

Boyd hadn't even heard this song when they began recording it, as it hadn't been written for guitar and Nick had refused to sing it a capella for him. In his sleeve notes to the *White Bicycles* compilation album, Boyd wrote of the "relief and joy" he and John Wood felt when they heard this music emerging from the speakers in their control booth, describing it as "a magnificent moment". Kirby's arrangement is heavenly, and has an aura of Bach to it. The references here to "sun" and "blue" seem to bear out Ian MacDonald's theories; there's real spiritual yearning here, and a quest for meaning in which the singer is willing to learn from anyone who might be able to teach him. Am I alone in hearing echoes of Simon Dupree's 1967 hit 'Kites' in this?

## DAY IS DONE

*Nick Drake, vocal and acoustic guitar; Robert Kirby, string arrangement.*

This was the first song that Kirby arranged, and he's subsequently admitted that he was very influenced by George Martin's work on The Beatles' 'Eleanor Rigby'. There's an air of pessimism here, of regret and weariness that today's tasks will inevitably carry over until tomorrow. The line "You sped the ball across the court" quoted on lyric sheets is a mishearing; what Nick actually sings is: "Newspaper blown across the court". It still sounds as if the image is one of a deserted tennis court, which Patrick Humphries has suggested could have been inspired by the ending of Antonioni's 1966 film *Blow Up*. The song has also been covered by Norah Jones.

## CELLO SONG

*Nick Drake, vocal and acoustic guitar; Clare Lowther, cello;*
*Danny Thompson, bass; Rocki Dzidzornu, congas.*

A song in praise of innocence, with the singer feeling unworthy of his love; she's far above him. There's a mournful quality here, though much of that is probably the simple result of using a cello.

## THE THOUGHTS OF MARY JANE

*Nick Drake, vocal and acoustic guitar; Robert Kirby, string arrangement.*

'Mary Jane' was fairly archaic slang for marijuana, dating back to the Fifties or earlier (in 1968 The Beatles recorded a nonsensical song of John Lennon's called 'What's The New Mary Jane', which was almost included on The White Album; it was finally released in 1996 on *Anthology 3*). However, this sounds much more like a love song to a girl than a song in praise of getting stoned. It's been suggested that Nick may be referring to Robin Frederick here, and she certainly indulged in Mary Jane herself (as she admitted in her song 'Been Smokin' Too Long', Nick's recording of which can be found on *Time Of No Reply*).

## MAN IN A SHED

*Nick Drake, vocal and acoustic guitar; Danny Thompson, bass;*
*Paul Harris, piano.*

An annoyingly meandering jazzy number about love across class barriers; the singer is in love with a girl much richer than himself, who wants to just remain a friend. This may tell us something about Nick's love life, but it's by far the weakest track here.

## FRUIT TREE

*Nick Drake, vocal and acoustic guitar; Robert Kirby, string arrangement.*

A song about finding posthumous fame, which now seems chillingly prophetic. The singer sees the world as a "theatre full of sadness"; Nick's own sadness sprang from the fact that he didn't know how to change it. Even so, there's no feeling of self-pity here (more a that's-the-way-the-world-is philosophical shrug), or any indication that Nick is talking of his own future (it certainly wasn't the future he was hoping for). There's a real Beatles influence evident, and also an echo of calypso. The song was included on the TV show spin-off album *Heartbeat: Number One Love Songs Of The 60s* in 1996, which sold over 300,000 copies.

## SATURDAY SUN

*Nick Drake, vocal and piano; Danny Thompson, bass; Tristan Fry, drums and vibraphone.*

Another song of wistful nostalgia – if Ian MacDonald is correct, Nick is pining for the happiness he knew in Aix. There's also another clear reference to reincarnation here (mislaid friends will all return in the end), and the inevitability of change. Nick plays some excellent bluesy piano here, and one wishes he'd recorded more in this vein – you could almost imagine Mose Allison recording this. The song was also covered by Alexis Korner on his eponymous 1971 album.

# Bryter Layter

*Island ILPS 9134 (LP); IMCD 71 (CD); released November 1970.*
*Produced by Joe Boyd. All compositions by Nick Drake.*

In October 1969, Nick moved into a room in Hills Road, Cambridge, and commenced his third year as a student. But in the middle of that month he wrote to his tutor Ray Kelly and formally announced his intention to leave Cambridge "to devote myself to my musical career". If Nick had stayed on for another nine months he would have been able to take his degree exams (which he'd probably have got), but neither Kelly nor Nick's parents could make him change his mind, though they spent weeks trying. Nick obviously believed his "musical career" was about to take off. Sadly, this wasn't the case; in fact, *Five Leaves Left* is thought to have sold less than 3,000 copies on its initial release. Nick nevertheless wanted to promote the album and to commence work on the follow-up. He moved to London, bouncing from sofa to sofa around the capital; living in Battersea and then Kensington with Gabrielle, sharing a flat in Notting Hill with a female friend and her pet monkey, staying with other friends in flats in Chelsea and Earls Court.

Since Nick was usually impossible to track down, Boyd insisted that he move into a place that actually had a phone, and financially assisted him to do so. Nick rented a garden flat in a large Victorian house in Haverstock Hill, Hampstead, which was vast and bare and freezing in the winter. Here he played guitar and smoked hashish, and seemed to do very little else; he certainly never decorated or furnished his spartan abode. Molly Drake dates the move to Hampstead as the point when the "shadows closed in" on her son. Up until then, no one really thought there was a serious problem with Nick's mental state. He was admittedly shy, but he had plenty of friends and liked parties, was almost universally liked by girls...

In the past he'd always compartmentalised his friends, keeping his London and Cambridge acquaintances apart. Now his social circle shrunk drastically. He'd accompany Joe Boyd to the home of Witchseason associate Bob Squire to play Liar Dice, would go to Tanworth to see his parents, and often visited John and Beverley Martyn, who lived nearby. And that was about it, and even with himself and the Martyns, Boyd noted, Nick was "guarded and quiet". At some point in early 1970 he became ill, suffering from kidney stones for which he was prescribed painkillers (which may well have affected his mental state).

As for gigging, Nick had reluctantly played a few dates on the folk club circuit – at Bunjie's, the Troubadour and Cousins – but he didn't exactly bring the house down. He had absolutely no between-song patter, and barely made eye contact with audiences. He'd also played at the Coventry Apprentices Xmas Ball and/or the Nettlefold Nut & Bolt Apprentices Annual Dance (accounts vary). Here he encountered a fairly riotous and rowdy crowd and, according to some accounts, was upset by their behaviour; others claim he simply found it vaguely amusing.

Things moved up a gear on September 24, 1969, when Fairport Convention played a concert at the Royal Festival Hall to promote their new album *Liege & Lief*. It was also the band's first concert since their drummer Martin Lamble had been killed in a motorway crash, so public interest was high. Boyd chose two other Witchseason acts to support Fairport that night: John and Beverley Martyn came on second, while Nick opened the show. He played a mere four numbers before leaving the stage, and barely said a word to the audience.

It was like that everywhere he played. His sister claims Nick had an electrifying stage presence, but most witnesses claim the exact opposite. By all accounts Nick had been a confident performer during his Marlborough days, and had had no problems playing for friends in Cambridge; now he seemed crippled by nerves, or shyness, or both. In John Martyn's words, he was always "distinctly uncomfortable on stage". He didn't even adapt his songs to a solo performance, simply strumming away during the passages where the strings had been on the record. Perhaps he was now just reluctant to play without the strings; in a 1971 interview he told *Sounds'* Jerry Gilbert that his songs had been written "for records rather than performing", and that he'd only played "two or three concerts that felt right, and there was something wrong with all the others".

But the Royal Festival Hall gig had somehow convinced Boyd that Nick could cope with performing live, and so he ordered the singer off on a nationwide tour of universities and clubs two months later. It was disastrous. Nick's need to constantly retune his guitar between songs left audiences restless and irritable (Keith James, who today tours Britain playing Nick's songs in concert, uses three pre-tuned guitars to do so – but this was not an option for Nick who only owned one at this point). Nor did Nick have any friendly banter with which to win audiences over, so people talked and clinked glasses, and the noise level made Nick even more uncomfortable; it wasn't unknown for him to just give up and walk offstage. Had he been playing with a group of other musicians, as he'd done at the May Ball, Nick might have been able to deal with it; as it was, he felt naked and isolated, both onstage and on the road. Witchseason hadn't even thought to provide him with a driver or a guitar roadie (presumably because other folk singers managed without them, and they presumed that Nick could do likewise), so Nick had to drive himself to gigs, and when things went wrong he didn't even have anyone he could moan to.

The full list of gigs that Nick played is unknown, but definitely included The Haworth in Hull (supporting Mike Chapman); the Upper Room folk club in Harrow; the Guest, Keen & Nettlefold's Social Club in Smethwick (playing to steel workers); and Ewell Technical College (supporting Atomic Rooster and the Peter Gabriel-era Genesis). In February 1970 he supported John and Beverley Martyn at Queen Elizabeth Hall; in March he began a five-date tour supporting Sandy Denny's new band Fotheringay, playing 2,000-3,000-seater halls. After the third gig of the Fotheringay tour, Nick told Boyd that he didn't want to continue, and Boyd reluctantly accepted the situation. Nick did subsequently play a few more dates: at Bedford College in May (John Martyn and Graham Bond were also on the bill); he also appeared that month at an open-air concert in Yorkshire, where Free were the headlining act. His final gig took place on June 25, at Ewell Technical College, supporting Ralph McTell. Halfway through the song 'Fruit Tree' Nick suddenly stopped playing and left the stage, this time forever (though he may have made a few folk club appearances over the course of the next year, just to raise some cash).

Today, we're a little more aware of the fact that live performance is a very different animal to creative art, and thanks to video and the Internet, playing music live is nowhere near as essential as it once was in an artist's promotion. Nick was far from unique in finding touring and live performance hellish, and he probably couldn't see why he should have to play this game. He was almost certainly aware of the fact that Harry Nilsson, Leonard Cohen and Randy Newman (at this stage in their careers) never performed live, and that Brian Wilson no longer accompanied The Beach Boys on tour. But all of these American artists had the advantage of their music being actively promoted through nationwide airplay on FM radio stations, the equivalent to which simply didn't exist in Britain. The occasional play on a John Peel show was hardly a substitute, and Nick's decision not to play live couldn't help but mean that his record sales would suffer as a result. According to Gabrielle Drake, Island remained incredibly supportive of him despite this decision, and Nick was still paid a small weekly stipend.

Somewhere in the middle of all this, the French chanteuse Francoise Hardy professed herself to be a fan of Nick's first album. There was talk of some kind of collaboration, and Nick went with Boyd to have tea with Hardy at her Paris apartment, during which Nick "barely uttered a word". The collaboration came to nothing, but Nick is said to have visited Hardy when she was recording in London, and saw her on at least one other occasion in Paris. (He tried to visit her on another occasion, but she was out; Nick supposedly fled without leaving a message when her maid answered the door.) All of which led to rumours of a romance between the two, which seems highly unlikely (though not impossible).

In early 1970, Nick travelled to Little Hadham near Bishop's Stortford, where Fairport Convention were living in a converted pub named The Angel. He stayed there for three or four days, rehearsing the new songs he had written at Haverstock Hill during the autumn of 1969 with the three members of Fairport that Boyd had lined up to play on

Nick's second album: guitarist Richard Thompson, bassist
Dave Pegg (who would later serve a spell in the ranks of
Jethro Tull) and drummer Dave Mattacks. This time the
material was about life in the big city, and – according to
Robert Kirby – despite Nick's evident unease at some aspects
of city dwelling, his intention was to make a "happy record".

*Bryter Layter* took eight or nine months to record, once
again at Sound Techniques. As well as the three Fairporters,
session players included flautist Lyn Dobson (from the Soft
Machine), alto sax player Ray Warleigh (who had played
not only with British jazzers such as Humphrey Lyttelton
and Ronnie Scott, but also with Long John Baldry, John
Mayall and Georgie Fame) and two Americans from The
Beach Boys' touring band: drummer Mike Kowalski and
bass player Ed Carter. Kowalski later stated that Nick was
"very much in control" of the sessions, happy for musicians
to improvise – but only up to a point. He also recalls the
tracks he worked on requiring "quite a few takes". Repris-
ing their roles from *Five Leaves Left* were pianist Paul Harris
and arranger Robert Kirby. Kirby had expected to become
a music teacher after leaving Cambridge; instead, his work
on Nick's first album had led to more orchestration work,
for Al Stewart, Ralph McTell, Dave Cousins and others.
*Bryter Layter* required Kirby to arrange for brass as well as
strings; he's since admitted that Van Morrison's *Astral Weeks*
was a big influence on his work here (as was Henry Purcell).

Also on board was the maverick classicist (and co-founder
of The Velvet Underground), John Cale, who was then in
London finishing work on Nico's *Desertshore* album, which
he was co-producing with Joe Boyd; during this period he
also played on Mike Heron's Boyd-produced solo album
*Smiling Men With Bad Reputations*. When Cale heard some
of the early tapes for *Bryter Layter,* he insisted on going off to
meet Drake that very day. In his autobiography, Boyd

relates that he got a phone call from Cale the next morning, saying, "We're going to need a pick-up for the viola, an amp, a Fender bass and bass amp, a celeste and a Hammond B-3 organ. This afternoon." Cale arrived at the studio followed by a somewhat bemused Nick. In Cale's autobiography he recalls that he "assisted Nick Drake on quite a few cuts on more than one of his albums", but it would seem his memory is faulty, and that 'Fly' and 'Northern Sky' were the only tracks he worked on. He did, however, introduce Drake to a new instrument, as he recalled in 2007: "I had a Martin D-12 12-string guitar and he'd never seen one before. He just picked up that guitar and it was just like this orchestral sound coming out. He went nuts, entranced. And all those chords are ringing. It was watching somebody get lost in an instrument. I didn't know about all the other problems, he was just very shy and very withdrawn. And I was trying to work out what the choruses were, but there weren't any." Nick subsequently bought himself a Martin D28 guitar, to supplement his trusty Guild F-20.

Dave Pegg later called the *Bryter Layter* sessions "one of the most memorable and enjoyable" times he'd ever spent in a recording studio. "Most of it was done live, and it was done fairly quickly," he added. But all of the album's main participants – Cale, Richard Thompson, Dave Pegg, Danny Thompson – have commented that Nick was so quiet throughout that he was impossible to talk to, and none of them were at all sure if he was happy with the results of their work or not. But Kirby recalls that once *Bryter Layter* was completed Nick was happy, confident and optimistic: "I think he felt this was going to be the one." So did Joe Boyd, who was confident that the whole approach this time was much more commercial; even so, Boyd had the feeling – although Nick never said it out loud – that the singer felt *Bryter Layter* was overarranged and overproduced.

The title *Bryter Layter* was of course a much-used phrase on TV weather reports, though it at least conveyed a sense of optimism; substituting a 'y' for an 'i' was for some reason common practice from the mid-Sixties onwards, as in The Byrds and The Cyrcle. The album sleeve was luridly coloured in mauve, red and orange (very Seventies), with a photograph by Keith Morris on the rear and a moody portrait of Nick by Nigel Waymouth on the front. When the record was first released, there was very little media interest in it. Nick was offered a TV spot on BBC2's 'progressive' rock show *Disco 2* (the forerunner of *The Old Grey Whistle Test*), but much to Island's annoyance he never showed up for the recording session. When the record failed to sell, Island decided to repromote it in March 1971. This time it attracted good reviews from Lon Goddard in *Record Mirror* and from Jerry Gilbert in *Sounds* (who called it "a superb album"). In the wake of this Nick gave his only interview, to Gilbert, but it was like getting blood from a stone, Nick's replies being mainly "monosyllabic", apart from the comments about public performance already quoted here.

Of all the numerous albums he produced, Joe Boyd still counts *Bryter Layter* as one of his all-time personal favourites, and would doubtless have still made the record regardless of any sales factor. He and John Wood "mixed it over and over until we were absolutely satisfied." It shows; the result is, quite simply, wonderful.

## INTRODUCTION

*Nick Drake, acoustic guitar; Dave Pegg, bass; Dave Mattacks, drums; Robert Kirby, string arrangement.*

The album opens with the first of its three instrumentals. Far from treating them merely as filler, Nick is said to have worked as hard on these as on any of his songs. On this one, Kirby's sweeping strings and Mattacks' solemn drumming create an air of yearning and aspiration – but it's incredibly brief (a minute and a half), and simply a scene setter.

## HAZEY JANE II

*Nick Drake, vocal and acoustic guitar; Dave Pegg, bass; Dave Mattacks, drums; Richard Thompson, lead guitar; Robert Kirby, brass arrangement.*

A drastic change of tempo, the words spilling out of Nick as if he's trying to keep pace with the insistent horns (which sound somewhat like the way The Beatles used horns during their psychedelic period); his breathy vocals still sound positively joyous. The song seems to be about the transient nature of life, as friends are left behind on the road, although there would also seem to be a reference to over-population (or simply the claustrophobic nature of life in a city that's as densely packed as the lyrics of this song). Slowing things down is the only way to stay sane, with a grass-roots approach to changing the world: begin with your brother and your sister (and by implication, yourself). Trevor Dann thinks 'Hazey Jane' might stand for heroin, in the same way that 'Mary Jane' stood for marijuana. Personally, I'm not convinced – and the other 'Hazey Jane' song on this album is definitely a love song to a girl, so the theory simply collapses. Here, 'Jane' is someone the singer is definitely pining for, but that doesn't mean she's a drug.

## AT THE CHIME OF A CITY CLOCK

*Nick Drake, vocal and acoustic guitar; Dave Pegg, bass; Mike Kowalski, drums; Ray Warleigh, alto sax; Robert Kirby, string and brass arrangement.*

A vaguely jazzy song about the big city and failing to fit in there. There are images of alienation and isolation and panic attacks ("the beads around your face" are beads of sweat), and curiously medieval images of self-defence (crown, armour) – yet these are all offset by the yearning beauty of the arrangement, which reprises the string theme of 'Introduction'. Nor is the message a bleak one – salvation is possible, and lies in the hope of finding a partner, then escaping from the city with your "bride" (even if this is sheer fantasy, it's a necessary one if one is to stay sane). Ian MacDonald has pointed out chord resemblance between this song and Cream's 'Deserted Cities Of The Heart' (from *Wheels Of Fire*) and also their cover of Skip James's 'I'm So Glad' (from *Fresh Cream*), and there is a definite resemblance. The song was also covered by The High Llamas on their 1997 album *Hawaii*.

## ONE OF THESE THINGS FIRST

*Nick Drake, vocal and acoustic guitar; Ed Carter, bass; Mike Kowalski, drums; Paul Harris, piano.*

It's unlikely that this is another reincarnation song, as some have claimed. It seems simply to be about indecision, about blowing possibilities – and a relationship – through a fear of failure (or a fear of success). The singer is prevented by his own nature from getting his act together; in a very real sense, he's lost, but making no excuses for himself. Ed Carter played Mike Kowalski's 1954 Fender Precision bass on this track, and Harris's piano playing is a delight. In 1971 the track was included on the Island Records sampler *El Pea*.

## HAZEY JANE I

*Nick Drake, vocal and acoustic guitar; Dave Pegg, bass; Dave Mattacks, drums; Robert Kirby, string arrangement.*

Some extraordinary guitar picking from Nick on this epic song about commitment (and the lack of it). If this is actually about heroin, I just can't see it. In 1970 the track was included on the Island Records sampler *Bumpers*.

## BRYTER LAYTER

*Nick Drake, acoustic guitar; Dave Pegg, bass; Dave Mattacks, drums; Lyn Dobson, flute; Robert Kirby, string arrangement.*

The album's second instrumental. There are those who think this sounds like elevator muzak, which is unfair; there are also those who think it sounds like a TV theme, which is a little closer to the truth. Dobson's vaguely jazzy flute weaves in and out of the soaring strings, on a tune that gets right inside your head and takes up permanent residence (flutes were big at the time, employed by Traffic, Jethro Tull, Quintessence and several other bands).

## FLY

*Nick Drake, vocal and acoustic guitar; John Cale, viola and harpsichord; Dave Pegg, bass.*

Nick is practically begging for a second chance here, asking for commitment while also placing his love on a pedestal.

"Streetcar by the bay" conjures up images of San Francisco, or some sunny seaside resort, ie it's another fantasy of escape. Cale's haunting arrangement of the song wouldn't have sounded out of place on his own *Vintage Violence* or *Paris 1919*, and I mean that as a compliment.

## POOR BOY

*Nick Drake, vocal and acoustic guitar; Dave Pegg, bass; Mike Kowalski, drums; Ray Warleigh, alto sax; Chris McGregor, piano; Pat Arnold and Doris Troy, backing vocals.*

Recorded one afternoon, after Boyd had spent the morning producing a session by the Chris McGregor Sextet; McGregor had stayed on to listen to Nick play. When Pegg and Kowalski began rehearsing the song with Nick – and with the sound of McGregor's piano playing fresh in his ears – it seemed to Boyd as if a touch of McGregor was just what the song needed. So, after a brief rehearsal, this jazzy outing was recorded in just one take, and Nick's vocal phrasing responds well to that of McGregor's piano. In his sleeve notes to the *White Bicycles* compilation album Boyd commented: "The chance meeting of two of the greatest musicians I ever worked with is one of my favourite moments in the studio." Boyd also chose to use two female backing singers, inspired by the way Leonard Cohen had used female singers on his debut album. Doris Troy was a soul singer who'd worked with Solomon Burke, The Drifters and Dionne Warwick, and who later did sessions for Dusty Springfield, The Rolling Stones and Pink Floyd. She died in 2004. Pat Arnold is better known as P.P. Arnold (of 'First Cut Is The Deepest' and 'Angel Of The Morning' fame), at this point working mainly as a session singer.

The song is about self-pity, though there's at least some

degree of self-mocking involved; then again, much of this mockery results from the arrangement, which Nick is thought to have been less than enthusiastic about (it does get irritating after a while), and Trevor Dann claims the demo version is much bleaker. The song carries the album's second reference to a bride; since Nick doesn't appear to have been seriously involved with anyone, this is probably yet another fantasy of escape. Ian MacDonald thought the line "nobody spreads their aching heads" was comparing people unfavourably to trees (about which Nick had a real passion).

## NORTHERN SKY

*Nick Drake, vocal and acoustic guitar; John Cale, celeste, piano and organ; Dave Pegg, bass; Mike Kowalski, drums.*

Over 30 years later, the *NME* called this the "greatest English love song of recent times", and it really does convey the joy and nervous excitement of falling (hard) for someone new, with Cale's delicate arrangement cradling Nick's hesitant optimism. Beverley Martyn has claimed that the song was written at her home in Hastings, and that the room Nick used to stay in there had a view of the ocean through the trees.

## SUNDAY

*Nick Drake, acoustic guitar; Dave Pegg, bass; Dave Mattacks, drums; Ray Warleigh, flute; Robert Kirby, string arrangement.*

The album closes with another instrumental, with Warleigh's mournful flute virtually carrying the almost medieval tune. Lon Goddard's *Record Mirror* review of *Bryter Layter* compares it to Mason Williams' 'Classical Gas' (a chart hit in 1969). Williams may or may not have been an influence, but it certainly sounds like it on this track.

# Pink Moon

*Island ILPS 9184 (LP); IMCD 94 (CD); released February 1972.*
*Produced by John Wood. All compositions by Nick Drake. All songs feature Nick Drake on vocal and acoustic guitar; he also plays piano on the title track.*

In early 1971, Joe Boyd felt that his Witchseason artists no longer needed him in the way that they once had. He'd disagreed with Fairport Convention about track selection for their *Full House* album, had drifted away from The Incredible String Band after they became Scientologists, and was annoyed with Sandy Denny for refusing to make a solo album. As for Nick, even before *Bryter Layter* was released he'd adamantly stated that he wanted his next record to be a lot simpler, and probably a solo effort. On top of all this, Witchseason was in debt. So when Boyd was offered a good job with Warner Brothers' film music department in California, he eagerly accepted. Before leaving Britain he sold Witchseason to Chris Blackwell, and paid off his creditors. One condition of the sale was that Nick's records should never be deleted, to which Blackwell – a fan of Nick's himself – happily agreed.

But Nick had relied heavily on Boyd, who'd been both a father figure and a mentor to him. Now, understandably, he felt abandoned. In retrospect, it seems strange that no one

suggested to Nick that he should find himself another manager; even if he was incapable of locating one himself, Chris
Blackwell could surely have advised him. Meanwhile, Boyd
and his girlfriend, the singer Linda Peters, had attempted to
keep their relationship going despite living on opposite sides
of the Atlantic; after a couple of months they realised the
distance was too great an obstacle, and parted. Later that
year Linda briefly dated Nick; although it didn't work out as
a romance, the two remained friends. Over the course of
1971 and 1972, she observed him becoming more and more
introverted, to an almost extreme degree ("almost like a
kind of autism").

Perhaps facing a financial crunch, Nick had left Haverstock
Hill to live in a succession of bedsits in London – the last of
them in Muswell Hill, 100 yards away from where Robert
Kirby was living. Finally, he left London for good, and
returned home to his parents in Tanworth. Nick had taken
the poor sales of his records personally, and told his mother:
"I've failed at everything I've tried to do." His parents were
deeply concerned about his state of mind, and wanted him
to see a psychiatrist; but Nick was worried that everyone
would assume he was crazy if he did. Molly persuaded him
to seek advice from Joe Boyd, and Nick duly telephoned Joe
in California. Boyd assured him that his parents' suggestion
was a sensible idea, and thought Nick sounded frightened.
Perhaps as a result of this conversation, Nick did consult with
a psychiatrist, at St Thomas's Hospital in London; what
resulted from this session is unknown, but it's not thought
that Nick was prescribed any medication at this stage.

Chris Blackwell lent Nick his Spanish villa for a brief hol-
iday, which helped a little – but Nick would remain living
at Far Leys for the rest of his days. He told his mother, "I
don't like it at home, but I can't bear it anywhere else." Still,
he went driving almost every day, sometimes aimless jaunts,

sometimes trips to see the Martyns in Hastings, John Wood in Suffolk, Brian Wells in Eastbourne or Sophia Ryde in London. He could be gone for hours or days at a time, and frequently ran out of petrol in the middle of nowhere (necessitating rescue by family or friends). On occasion he'd turn up at the offices of Island or Witchseason, and would sit there for hours, just reading a newspaper.

In October 1971 Nick called John Wood and told him that he was ready to record his next album, and wanted Wood to act as his producer. Since Sound Techniques was booked solidly during daylight hours, the decision was made to record at night, during the studio's dead time, rather than delay the project or find another studio. In the end *Pink Moon* took two nights to record. The sessions began at midnight, and the songs truly sound as if they belong to the wee small hours. There was only one overdub – this being Nick's piano part on the title track. Linda Peters visited Nick in the studio during the sessions, only to discover that he wouldn't talk to her; he wouldn't even talk to John Wood. When Nick announced that he was completely finished, Wood was surprised that there were no more songs to add (the album is a mere 26 minutes in length), and equally amazed that Nick wanted absolutely nothing added to the tracks. They were what they were. A day or so later Nick delivered the master tape of the album to Island Records in person. Despite the popular myth that he left the tape in the care of a receptionist and promptly disappeared, Nick actually saw Chris Blackwell that day. Blackwell asked what the album's studio costs had been, and promptly settled up with Nick on the spot (a mere £500, according to Blackwell).

Rodney Drake has stated that Nick was "very down" when he wrote the songs for *Pink Moon*, but in fact no one is too sure where and when the songs were written. Robert Kirby recognised guitar phrases and fragments that Nick had been toying with back in his Cambridge days, and several others have stated that many of the songs date back to 1969 or thereabouts. Some find the album bleak and depressing, but it really isn't. It's undeniably stark and spare, but that's a part of its beauty – and if Nick was in a depressed and confused state of mind, it certainly doesn't show in the music; he's at his peak as a guitarist here. Some of the songs are bluesy and bleak, but others are truly joyous; some can be read either way, and there's far more wistful sadness on display than true existential angst (just compare any of the songs here with 'Black Eyed Dog', and you'll see what I mean). Overall, though, the theme is one of triumph and redemption, ending in the exultant mystical celebration of 'From The Morning'.

Keith Morris was once again commissioned to photograph Nick for the album cover (and was shocked at the change in his subject since the *Bryter Layter* sessions). In the end, Island chose not to use any of Morris's photographs, opting instead to commission a surreal painting for the album's cover; the artist was Michael Trevithick, a friend of Gabrielle Drake's.

In the long run, *Pink Moon* proved to be the biggest selling of Nick's three studio albums (*Five Leaves Left* came second), but the reviews in *Melody Maker* and *Sounds* were both distinctly unenthusiastic. And the world into which *Pink Moon* was released was a grim and bleak one. In Britain there had been a long, cold winter of power cuts (caused by a miners' strike), which was merely the beginning of ongoing industrial unrest on a massive scale (within a year Britain would become a part-time nation, as these problems led to the institution of the government-enforced three-day working week). The idealism of the hippie years (by then reduced to cliché and generally dismissed) had been replaced by the polysexual hedonism of glam-rock, and hard drugs abounded; the key phrases of the year were "a bit of the old ultraviolence" and "divine decadence" (from *A Clockwork Orange* and *Cabaret* respectively). Richard Nixon was the US President (and would be re-elected in a landslide victory later in the year), and the Vietnam War still ground on, with no end in sight. In short, it was a particularly bad time to be suffering from depression.

## PINK MOON

A pink moon can be a beautiful sight, if it's the by-product of a spectacular sunset. But the image that comes to mind more readily is that of a lunar eclipse, when the shadow of the Earth makes the moon appear to go a reddish colour. Traditionally, the sight is an ill omen, and a harbinger of death (according to most astrologers, people can die or undergo other dramatic transformative events during an eclipsed full moon in their own birth sign). It could also be seen as referring to Monday; and in Nick's symbology, if Saturday was happy and Sunday was sad, then Monday was as bad as it can get. The moon as a symbol of death makes more sense here that MacDonald's theory that it stands for illusion; after all, it's "gonna get ye all".

Yet there's nothing dark or doom-laden here, more an acceptance that's somewhere between philosophical and joyful. As many have pointed out, there seems to be a strong John Martyn influence here. There's also Nick's stunning piano playing, which makes one wish that he'd recorded a whole album in this vein. The song was also used as the soundtrack for a TV commercial advertising the Volkswagen Cabrio in the late Seventies. According to Trevor Dann, in the month following the ad's first screening Nick sold more records in the USA that he had in the previous three decades put together. The song was also covered by Walt Mink on his 1992 album *Miss Happiness*.

## PLACE TO BE

Thought to date back to 1969, and perhaps earlier. It's a bluesy ballad concerning Nick's quest for happiness via a romantic relationship, in which he's having to force himself to keep going. But it's more about weariness and minor-league self-pity than actual despair.

## ROAD

Some think this is about survival, some think it's about contemplating suicide. You pays your money… but it seems to me that there's some gritty determination on display here, so the former gets my vote. Nick's playing here is absolutely hypnotic.

## WHICH WILL

Another song in the vein of many on *Bryter Layter*, asking for some sign of commitment from a prospective partner. The song was later covered by Lucinda Williams.

## HORN

Ian MacDonald has suggested that this brief and delicate guitar instrumental was influenced by Indian veena music; Trevor Dann hears a North African influence instead, presumably planted during Nick's days in Morocco. I'm more inclined to agree with MacDonald, though the influence could just as easily be Spanish (and Nick *had* just been to Spain). Horn was also the name of a Cambridge jazz group who shared the bill with Nick at the 1969 May Ball.

## THINGS BEHIND THE SUN

Thought to date back to 1968, or even earlier (Nick performed it live at the Queen Elizabeth Hall in February 1969). Some think this is about drugs, which is unlikely. It seems to be simply about not fitting in with the modern world and its materialist beliefs and aspirations – and of being proud of that ("To win the Earth just won't seem worth your night or your day"), since those more worldly are scarcely to be envied ("Say a prayer for people there"). Joe Boyd had wanted Nick to include this song on *Bryter Layter*, but the singer refused, determined to keep it for his "no frills" project.

Musically and lyrically, this one is a lot more upbeat than people usually give it credit for, and its core message ("be what you'll be") is a deeply positive one.

## KNOW

A mournful, gorgeous blues that shows the influence of Robert Johnson, its minimal lyric a masterpiece of romantic ambivalence and confusion. Trevor Dann accurately points out its similarity to the Doors' 'Roadhouse Blues', which had been released the year before (but then again, Nick was known to dislike Jim Morrison, so it may just be sheer coincidence).

## PARASITE

Another song about not fitting in, which is thought to date back to 1969. This could be seen as revealing of Nick's low self-esteem, or even self-loathing – yet it could also be mockingly ironic, in the same way as 'Poor Boy'. It's more likely that Nick is simply talking about not truly belonging to city life, merely clinging on and getting by. In short, it's about alienation but, as with 'Things Behind The Sun', there's also compassion for others expressed here ("Who's to care if they lose"). When Nick was living in Haverstock Hill, his local underground station would have been Chalk Farm, which is indeed on the Northern Line. It also has stairs, but Nick's reference to "sailing downstairs" suggests an escalator to me.

## RIDE

Sometimes also called 'Free Ride'. According to Trevor Dann, shortly before recording *Pink Moon* Nick asked Sophia Ryde to type up some of his handwritten lyrics. It seemed to her that this song clearly referred to her, since she had a small collection of post-impressionist paintings, and that the title could also be seen as a play on her surname. If true, then Nick's request was a far from subtle way of shoving his message right under her nose. As far as the lyric goes, Nick is telling his love that he's worth far more than her wealthy lifestyle ("A carpet that's so thick on the floor") or her high-society friends. The song was covered by Tir Na Nog on their 1973 album *Strong In The Sun*, and was given extensive radio play at the time.

## HARVEST BREED

Does "the end" refer to the end of a relationship, the end of the line, the end of life itself? It doesn't sound gloomy enough to be any of these, yet that could just be down to Nick's acceptance of his situation – and the last line does almost conjure up a *Wicker Man*-style pagan sacrifice… although harvest time is more usually a cause for celebration.

## FROM THE MORNING

The album closes with redemption; a song of taking pleasure in nature's beauty, of real optimism for the future. The ending is a mystical vision of triumph (though whether in this life or not is debatable), and the saddest thing in evidence here is Nick's faltering vocal, as if he's running out of fuel. The line "Now we rise, and we are everywhere" is inscribed on the back of Nick's gravestone.

# Time Of No Reply

*Hannibal Records HNBL 1318 (LP); HNCD 1318 (CD),
released August 1986 as part of* Fruit Tree, *and in its own right
in March 1987.*
*Produced by Frank Kornelussen and Joe Boyd. All compositions
by Nick Drake except 'Been Smoking Too Long' (credited on the
sleeve as 'author unknown', the song was later revealed to be the
work of Robin Frederick).*

*P*ink Moon made little impact upon the world, and with
its release Nick's contract with Island is thought to have
lapsed; this would have meant an immediate end to his
stipend from the label. Several months later, he had a nervous breakdown. At his GP's suggestion, Nick was admitted
for observation to Barnsley Hall psychiatric hospital in
Bromsgrove, where he stayed for five weeks. While there
he was prescribed three sets of pills: the antidepressant
Tryptizol, the tranquilliser Stelazine and Disipal (which
counteracted some of the side effects of the Stelazine). This
was an era when Valium was still being doled out to
depressed housewives like Smarties as the standard quick-fix
solution to their problems; the same may be true today of
Prozac, but at least now people are more aware of alterna-
tive treatment options to the purely pharmaceutical ones.

Dr Brian Wells told Trevor Dann that if he encountered
a patient with Nick's symptoms today, he would suggest

treating them with cognitive behavioural therapy rather than with drugs: "I would send them to an experiential treatment centre, where you climb ropes and mix with people and get some confidence." Sadly, all Nick got was the pills. At first they seemed to help, but before too long a whole range of unpleasant side effects kicked in as well: torpor and absent-mindedness, memory loss and dramatic mood swings, as well as physical twitches and tremors. Nick went steadily downhill.

All Nick's friends were deeply concerned. Some visited him at Far Leys, but Nick wasn't easy to talk to. He spent his time listening to music in his room, or driving aimlessly for hours around the countryside. He was now entering what Linda Thompson has referred to as "his Howard Hughes phase, which was really scary". He stopped washing, his clothes were dirty, his fingernails long and uncared for. The latter were a particularly upsetting sight, because Nick had always been scrupulously careful about his nails, as they affected his guitar playing. To Linda, the fact that he was now neglecting them was a sign that he was consciously avoiding playing the guitar at all. Perhaps so; Nick was suffering from writer's block, and no new music was filling his head. Ironically, Nick's music had just received its first American release, on Warners. The imaginatively titled *Nick Drake* album was compiled of tracks from *Five Leaves Left* and *Bryter Layter*, and had received a good review in *Rolling Stone*. Asylum's David Geffen later claimed that he'd been seriously interested in managing Nick, but that Island Records kept evading his enquiries.

At the beginning of 1974 Nick went to visit Joe Boyd, who'd now returned to Britain. Boyd was shocked by Nick's appearance – and by his uncharacteristic anger. Nick wanted to know why he'd been so unsuccessful, if he was truly so talented. Boyd explained that a few good reviews and a few radio plays on the John Peel show weren't enough to make Nick a star, and that his refusal to play live and general low profile certainly hadn't helped. In the end, Boyd did the only thing he could think of to cheer Nick up: he offered him the chance to make another record.

In February 1974 Nick went into the studio again with both Joe Boyd and John Wood; the session probably lasted only one day, but the trio returned to the studio again for a few days in July. The sessions were a bit of a trial for all concerned. Boyd felt that Nick's confidence and concentration were both badly shaken, since the faultless player of a few years before was now unable to sing and play at the same time without making mistakes. Boyd had to record the guitar part first, then Nick would overdub the vocals. The product of both sessions was a mere four songs: 'Rider On The Wheel', 'Black Eyed Dog', 'Hanging On A Star' and 'Voice From The Mountain'. (In 2004 a fifth song that everyone had forgotten, 'Tow The Line', surfaced on *Made To Love Magic*.) Nick had been a prolific songwriter early on in his career, but the process had gradually slowed to a crawl; he'd claimed that the reason *Pink Moon* was so short was simply because he'd run out of songs – and the fact that some of the songs on that album even pre-dated *Bryter Layter* says a lot, as does the fact that Nick was considering reviving some of his earliest unreleased songs for his fourth album. He had nothing else. At the end of the July sessions it seems probable that Boyd and Wood told Nick that they should take some more time off and then try again later.

It's been said that Nick was unhappy with the results of the two recording sessions, but Boyd was enthusiastic, and serious enough about the prospects of a new album to tell Nick that a new contract would soon be issued for him (presumably once again with Island). At some point that year Nick also made a tape of songs-in-progress at John

Wood's home studio; according to his parents, he was in very bad shape at the time. He told Wood that he was "dead inside" emotionally. Nick was depressed by news of two suicides that year: that of his musical hero, Graham Bond (who had thrown himself under a tube train), and that of his friend Julian Ormsby-Gore (who had hanged himself). Nick was aware of his personal decline, and bewildered by his own mental state. At one point, he supposedly seriously considered joining the army, but changed his mind. When he expressed an interest in becoming a computer programmer, his father managed to get him a job; but when it was discovered that he'd have to move back to London and live on his own again while taking a computer course, Nick simply disappeared for a few days, then never went back. He also cut his hair short and started wearing glasses all the time (he'd worn them for reading for years).

In late 1974 Nick went to Paris, and stayed with friends on a barge on the Seine near Notre Dame. This seems to have been a joyful time for him, although nobody knows the reasons why; and it wasn't all good, either. Francoise Hardy told Patrick Humphries that she'd met Nick during this trip and had dinner with him, in the course of which Nick was totally silent. Even so, when Nick returned from the trip, his parents thought him happier than he'd been for years; he even spoke enthusiastically about making music again

It wasn't to be. On the night of Sunday November 24, 1974, Nick went to bed early and listened to a recording of Bach's *Brandenburg Concertos*. He got up during the night to eat a bowl of cornflakes in the kitchen, which was by no means unusual – Nick frequently suffered from insomnia, which may well have been a side effect of the Stelazine he was taking. His other main prescription, Tryptizol, is often used as a sedative, and Nick may well have been told these pills would help him to sleep. That night, he took some more pills, though whether he was intending to kill himself or just trying to get some sleep is debatable. When he hadn't got up by noon the following day, his mother went to wake him and discovered his dead body lying across his bed, wearing only his underpants. As far as can be determined, he had died approximately six hours earlier, probably from a heart attack caused by an overdose of Tryptizol. He's thought to have taken approximately 30 tablets – somewhere between double and triple his daily dosage.

On his bedside table was a copy of the last book he was reading, *Le Mythe de Sisyphe* by Albert Camus. Since the book deals with suicide, there are some who point to its presence at the scene as evidence that Nick deliberately took his own life – yet the book is (in part) actually the existentialist argument *against* suicide. On Nick's desk were an exercise book containing all his handwritten lyrics and a letter to Sophia Ryde in a sealed envelope that he'd written the day before; she has never disclosed the contents of this letter, but one could make a guess: Nick was probably asking her for another chance, since she had recently ended their on/off relationship. There was no suicide note.

There was no post-mortem examination either, and Nick's body was quickly released for burial. His funeral took place on December 2 and was attended by around 50 of his friends from all the different 'compartments' of his life: Marlborough, Aix, Cambridge, high society, the music business. Nick was cremated at Solihull Crematorium, and his ashes were then buried in the graveyard of St Mary Magdalene church in Tanworth-in-Arden, not far from Far Leys. The inscription on his gravestone reads simply: "Nick Drake, 1948 – 1974. Remembered with love." On its reverse is inscribed a line from 'From The Morning': "Now we rise, and we are everywhere".

An inquest was held into Nick's death on December 18 and recorded a verdict of suicide, the cause being "acute Amitrypline poisoning self administered when suffering from a depressive illness". Many of Nick's closest friends questioned the suicide verdict, Joe Boyd, Robert Kirby and Brian Wells among them. They point to the fact that there were no real signs of a suicidal intent. John Wood's wife, Shirley, had once asked Nick why he hadn't simply committed suicide, since he was so depressed. "It's too cowardly," he'd told her, "and besides, I don't have the courage."

But according to Trevor Dann, Rodney and Molly Drake confided in Scott Appel that Nick had actually made one serious suicide bid the year before his death, when he'd attempted to hang himself at Far Leys but had been discovered and cut down in time. Whether this took place before or after his hospitalisation is unknown – but even if Nick had been truly suicidal at some point during 1973, it doesn't necessarily mean that he felt that way in November 1974.

Shortly after Nick's death, Jerry Gilbert penned a 600-word obituary for *Sounds* titled 'Death Of A Genius', but his passing was otherwise ignored by the media. A year later Nick Kent wrote a long appreciative piece about Nick in *NME*; titled 'Requiem For A Solitary Man', Kent's article challenged the suicide verdict, and also drew attention to the fact that there was unreleased Nick Drake material in Island's vaults. Yet for some reason, Island Records seemed to believe for several years that Nick's final four songs had been destroyed by John Wood because Nick hadn't been satisfied with them. By 1978 these four tracks had been located, and Island started to make plans for a boxed set of Nick's "complete collected works", ie the three studio albums plus the 'new' songs. When the project was first mooted, both Molly Drake and Joe Boyd independently came to the conclusion that there was only one possible title for this boxed set, and so it was agreed that it should be called *Fruit Tree* when it was released in March 1979, after the song that now seemed to have prophesied Nick's own fate. *Fruit Tree* was one of the very first boxed sets to retrospectively examine an artist's career, and it's a measure of the esteem in which Nick's music was held by Island that such a project was even considered. Nick Kent was commissioned to write sleeve notes, but these were rejected, as the tone Kent adopted wasn't thought to be appropriate for such an artefact; instead, American journalist Arthur Lubow contributed a long and thoughtful essay that covered most of the bare facts about Nick's life, and this was printed in a booklet that also included the lyrics to all Nick's songs (although these contain some errors) and numerous photographs.

*Fruit Tree* was deleted by Island in 1983. In 1985, Frank Kornelussen and Joe Boyd discovered the master tapes for most of Nick's recording sessions in Island's vaults. As a result, they uncovered some good unreleased material, and so – when the boxed set was reissued on Boyd's own Hannibal label in 1986 – these tracks were added to the 'final' four songs to make a whole 'new' album, *Time Of No Reply* (now a far sadder title than Nick had originally intended). The album was included in the new *Fruit Tree* box, and then released in its own right the following year.

## TIME OF NO REPLY

Thought to have been written in Aix-en-Provence in early 1967, and recorded at Sound Techniques in December 1968. The song was a staple of Nick's early live set (and was recorded by him for a John Peel session), to the point that many of Nick's friends were surprised that it wasn't included on *Five Leaves Left* (so am I, frankly). It's a song of lost love and regret, with some exquisite guitar work and a beautifully ethereal vocal. A faster solo version than this is also thought to exist.

## I WAS MADE TO LOVE MAGIC

The first of Nick's songs that Joe Boyd ever heard, also known at various times as 'Made To Love Magic' and simply 'Magic'. The orchestral arrangement here is by Richard Hewson, and this version was probably recorded in late 1968. It's mildly pleasant, but never really ignites (probably because of the arrangement). The song seems to be about loss of childhood innocence (a common theme in Nick's work, and in the hippie era in general), which Nick is proclaiming he alone has managed to retain – yet his solitary path is accepted calmly, and without self-pity. There are lines here in which Nick seems to acknowledge the inevitability of his eventual fate: "I was born to love no one/No one to love me", and also "I was born to sail away into a land of forever/Not to be tied to an old stone grave in your land of never". An early draft of the song included the line "many deaths ago", which is clearly another reincarnation reference.

## JOEY

Recorded in November 1968, and the best of three takes of the song (according to Kornelussen). It's a distinctly average love song about a contrary girl, and was possibly written about an Aix girlfriend, Jo D'Arcy. There's also another song about her, 'Joey In Mind', which remains unreleased. This one seems influenced by early Joni Mitchell, but is nowhere near as good. Judging by the handwritten lyric partially reproduced in the *Fruit Tree* booklet, there was originally an extra verse to this.

## CLOTHES OF SAND

Recorded in November 1968. The title 'Clothes Of Sand' appears on Nick's lyric sheet, but it may not have been his final choice for the song; in the session it was referred to only as 'New Song No. 2'. Kornelussen states in his sleeve notes that no one – including Boyd, Wood and Nick's parents – remembered this song at all. Although a love song of sorts, the dreamlike imagery here suggests more than a passing familiarity with hallucinogenic drugs ("to see the earth through painted eyes"). The song is also about impermanence, and the transitory nature of all things. Musically, this one conjures up early Joni Mitchell as well, and also suffers by the comparison.

## MAN IN A SHED

A solo acoustic take, recorded in October 1968 (earlier than the album version). It's better than the version on *Five Leaves Left*, but remains quite a weak song.

## MAYFAIR

Recorded in October 1968. One of Molly Drake's favourites of her son's songs, and it's intentionally very much in the vein of artists she admired, such as Noël Coward and Ivor Novello. Yet Nick is not glamourising this elegant upper-class enclave; he is very much an outsider who dislikes the fact that "beauty here is cold as ice" and "even trees are wealthy here". It's truly lovely, with Nick's jazzy strumming and delicate vocal adding to the irony of the piece; at one point he forgets the words and giggles. The song was also covered in 1970 by Millie (of 'My Boy Lollipop' fame), on an album produced and arranged by Robert Kirby.

## FLY

A demo version, recorded at Far Leys in 1969. This has slightly different lyrics to the final version. It's mildly interesting, but John Cale's arrangement of the song for *Bryter Layter* is much better.

## THE THOUGHTS OF MARY JANE

Recorded in December 1968 (earlier than the album version). Richard Thompson plays electric guitar here, contributing some jazzy noodling that's far below standard for him. This version has nothing else to recommend it over the version on *Five Leaves Left*.

## BEEN SMOKING TOO LONG

Recorded at Far Leys in 1967 or 1968 and written by American singer-songwriter Robin Frederick, with whom Nick became friends in Aix during 1967. She'd written this song the year before. It's a fairly pedestrian blues, blaming indulgence in cannabis for all of life's woes. Nick presumably agreed with the sentiment on occasion – although he changed the line "got the marijuana blues" to "got no other life to choose" (but another reference to "hash" remained unchanged).

## STRANGE MEETING II

Thought to have been written in Aix-en-Provence in early 1967, and recorded at Far Leys in 1967 or 1968. The title would seem to be a homage to Wilfred Owen's compassionate anti-war poem 'Strange Meeting', which concerns a conversation with a dead soldier – although Nick's song

'Bird Flew By' (see *Family Tree*) was also known as 'Strange Meeting I'. Here Nick encounters a mysterious "princess of the sand" – although this doesn't really ring true as a love song, more an exercise in fiction. Musically, it's a rather dull folk ballad.

## RIDER ON THE WHEEL

Recorded in February 1974. This seems to be a diatribe against the music business and the emptiness of fame, although the tone is more one of weary resignation than anything else. It's a likeable, bluesy little number that could easily have fitted on *Pink Moon*.

## BLACK EYED DOG

Recorded in February 1974. As previously noted, the blues singer Robert Johnson was a big influence on Nick. His friend Ben Lacock told journalist Mick Brown that Nick had once told him that, like Johnson, he too felt he had a hellhound on his trail. The result is this harrowing blues piece, which truly sounds like a cry for mercy. A black dog is actually an old symbol for the devil, and from the 18th century on had also been a phrase used to describe depression (most famously by Winston Churchill)... and of course, it also conjures up the image of Cerberus from Greek myth, standing at the gates of hell. It would seem that for Nick the dog here might represent death rather than depression; either way, he's tired and wants an end to his suffering ("I'm growing old and I wanna go home"). It's also another song in which Ian MacDonald discerned the influence of Indian veena music (and there are distinct similarities to 'Horn'). For all its darkness, a stunning, epic piece of work, with effortlessly dazzling blues guitar picking. The song was also later covered by Christine Collister.

## HANGING ON A STAR

Recorded in February 1974. A Dylanesque complaint against someone who'd let him down – perhaps Boyd for promising him success, or else a lover who wouldn't commit.

## VOICE FROM A MOUNTAIN

Thought to date back to 1969, and recorded in February or July 1974. It's a minor work but quite likeable; a mystical, nature-centred reverie.

# Made To Love Magic

*Island CID 8141 (CD); released 2004.*
*Produced by John Wood. All compositions by Nick Drake.*

On November 20, 1994 a memorial service for Nick was held in Tanworth to mark the 20th anniversary of his passing, attended by Gabrielle, now Nick's last surviving relative (Rodney had passed away in 1988, Molly in 1993, and their ashes were interred in the same grave where Nick's ashes lay). The ten years that followed saw Nick's popularity soar dramatically, fuelled by – among other things – the 'Pink Moon' Volkswagen advert, Patrick Humphries' biography and several compilation albums. At first glance, *Made To Love Magic* appears to be another one of these, with only one 'new' song – 'Tow The Line' – appearing on the menu; but in fact, all of the tracks here are either new versions or new mixes. Perhaps the most imaginative aspect of this album was the discovery of two of Robert Kirby's original arrangements that had never been recorded for *Five Leaves Left*. With some cunning digital reconstruction, new recordings of these arrangements were married to Nick's original vocals. The track listing here almost duplicates that of *Time Of No Reply*, but for those with limited funds *Made To Love Magic* would be a wiser investment, as it's an altogether more satisfying album. The accompanying booklet included several examples of Nick's handwritten lyrics. 'Magic' was also released as Nick's first ever single, and reached number 32 on the UK chart. The album itself would go on to become his best-selling CD (at the time of its release).

## RIDER ON THE WHEEL

When originally released, this track was mixed from a 7″ mono 'listening tape'. Here, the song has been properly mixed in true stereo by John Wood from the original multi-track tape.

## MAGIC

Robert Kirby's orchestral arrangements for both 'I Was Made To Love Magic' and 'Time Of No Reply' were never recorded during the sessions for *Five Leaves Left*, merely written as music in manuscript form. In August 2003 this new arrangement was recorded, and Nick's vocal was digitally stripped out of the original recording and slightly sped up in tempo (without the pitch being altered). The result is statelier and less saccharine than Hewson's more leaden arrangement on *Time Of No Reply*, as a result of which the song itself is more likeable. The reason it wasn't recorded like this in the first place was apparently because Nick wanted only one song on *Five Leaves Left* on which an orchestra was his sole accompaniment, and 'Way To Blue' won out over this one.

## RIVER MAN

A solo demo version, recorded in Robert Kirby's room in Cambridge in spring 1968. You'd think that with the string arrangement removed this song would be rather dull; but the power of Nick's guitar drives it on, and it's as mesmerising as ever (even if you do find yourself mentally putting the strings back in place).

## JOEY

See *Time Of No Reply*. This version has been remastered.

## THE THOUGHTS OF MARY JANE

See *Time Of No Reply*. This version has been remastered.

## MAYFAIR

Another solo demo version recorded in Robert Kirby's room in Cambridge, during spring 1968. This is somewhat faster – and much better – than the version on *Time Of No Reply*.

## HANGING ON A STAR

A newly discovered version of the song, with a better (and angrier) vocal. Recorded in July 1974.

## THREE HOURS

Recorded at Morgan Studios in March 1969 (two months before the version of the song that appears on *Five Leaves Left*). Percussion is by 'Reebop' Kwaku Baah (who later joined Traffic) on congas; the identity of the flautist is unknown. Pretty good, if not quite as good as the version we already knew.

## CLOTHES OF SAND

See *Time Of No Reply*. This version has been remastered.

## VOICES

Aka 'Voice From The Mountain'. Details as for 'Rider On The Wheel' (above).

## TIME OF NO REPLY

Another new orchestral backing for an old track (see entry for 'Magic', above), also recorded in August 2003. Here, Kirby's arrangement has simply been added to Nick's guitar/vocal recording. It's decidedly subtle, letting the song breathe while gently enhancing it and improving it.

## BLACK EYED DOG

Details as for 'Rider On The Wheel' (above).

## TOW THE LINE

Rediscovered in 2003, this was supposedly the last song recorded by Nick at Sound Techniques during July 1974, although the song itself probably dates back to 1969.

It's a gentle guitar ballad, possibly about the frustrations of dealing with the music business, possibly about being messed about in a relationship. Judging by the lyrics 'tow the line' is a simple spelling mistake, rather than a pun. Nick's vocal is fragile and tentative, and he doesn't sound in the best of shape; the track ends with the clunk of his guitar being put down, as if for the last time.

# Family Tree

*Island 0-06025-1734041-1 (CD); released July 2007.*
*Songwriting credits as listed under each track.*

In the years following Nick's death, Rodney and Molly Drake had happily played host to a steady trickle of Nick's fans who'd come from all over the world to pay their respects to his grave and to visit his childhood home. The Drakes patiently answered questions about their son, showed visitors the music room at Far Leys (it says a lot about the Drakes as a family that they devoted a whole room exclusively to music), and were only too happy to give away cassette copies of Nick's home demo recordings and photostats of his handwritten lyrics to fans. Inevitably, some irreplaceable items were lost over the years – and equally inevitably, a copy of the tape made its way into the hands of the unscrupulous, and bootlegs began to surface on the market during the Nineties. Gabrielle Drake was very unhappy about this situation, since the bootlegs were usually of very poor sound quality (often taken from third- or fourth-generation copies of the original tape), and she doubtless feared that they might tarnish Nick's legacy. Meanwhile, Nick's profile had continued to rise; media interest fuelled by Patrick Humphries' biography and *Made To Love Magic* led to the broadcast of TV and radio documentaries about Nick, and the publication of a new biography, Trevor Dann's *Darker Than The Darkest Sea.*

In 2007, Gabrielle finally decided to release an album of Nick's home recordings – although by now there was more material to draw on than just the tapes that Nick had recorded at Far Leys during 1967 and 1968. A tape he had recorded in April or May 1967 during his stay in Aix En Provence had surfaced in the late Nineties, which was promptly acquired by the Drake Estate. The material on both the Aix and Far Leys tapes consisted of a wide variety of cover versions, as well as Nick's own very early songs. The *Family Tree* album would also include two tracks recorded by Robert Kırby in Cambridge in 1968 (this tape had been long mislaid by Kirby, but had resurfaced in time to provide material for *Made To Love Magic*). Additionally, various oddities by Nick and other members of the Drake family were added, including two of Molly Drake's songs. Fans were now finally in a position to judge whether Molly had been a serious musical influence upon her son (as Joe Boyd thought when he first heard tapes of Molly singing, long after Nick's death). *Family Tree* was produced by the Drake Estate's manager, Cally, and all the tapes had been remastered by John Wood (though the tape quality on some tracks remains rather poor). The album was lovingly pack-aged with a booklet containing a collection of family snap-shots, reminiscences from Robert Kirby, Robin Frederick and Nick's childhood friend Andrew Hicks, as well as an open letter from Gabrielle Drake to her brother, explaining why she felt the need to release these recordings – though sadly, no lyrics were included.

As far as his own early songs go, it's worth noting that Nick himself chose not to record them for his debut album, possibly because Joe Boyd had advised against including any of them, possibly because Nick himself had simply tired of them or (correctly) thought them inferior to the songs he wrote later. However, it's also been rumoured that Nick was thinking of reviving some of them for inclusion on his fourth album; if true, it's probably a measure of how desperate he was for material then, rather than a measure of how good the songs are. That said, 'Bird Flew By' is a real gem.

Overall, *Family Tree* provides a fascinating glimpse of a budding young musician in the process of experimentation, trying out different styles while tentatively forging his own. It's also nice to hear the introductory fragments of Nick talking, and the interruptions when he's laughing at his own mistakes. Probably for completists only, but it still contains half a dozen or so items that genuinely enrich the Drake canon.

But *Family Tree* may not be quite the end of the story, as there still remains a small body of material left unreleased (see UNRELEASED WORKS), in addition to which there may well be other/alternate versions of known songs. There's also the snippet of Nick playing 'Plaisir D'Amour', currently available only on the compilation *Nick Drake: A Treasury*. Consequently, a second *Family Tree* collection remains a distinct possibility, though it would probably be a much slimmer volume; however, one can't help but suspect that if the Drake Estate ever intended to release this material at all, they would have included it here.

## COME IN TO THE GARDEN (INTRODUCTION)

*(Nick Drake)*

Recorded at Far Leys. A slow, mournful blues about a girl who goes her own way. All we're given here is the first verse, since a different take of the song follows later.

## THEY'RE LEAVING ME BEHIND

*(Nick Drake)*

Recorded in Aix en Provence, and thus one of Nick's very first original songs. It's a slow and somewhat despondent folk song about not fitting in anywhere, with the singer seemingly choosing to opt out of the rat race with the telling line, "Success can be gained, but at too great a cost." Musically, it sounds influenced by early Joni Mitchell, and also bears a resemblance to Nick's own 'One Of These Things First' (but is less tuneful, and nowhere near as good).

## TIME PIECE

*(Nick Drake)*

Recorded at Far Leys, date unknown. To a metronome backing, Nick recites a short poem about time, and sounds decidedly upper middle class.

## POOR MUM

*(Molly Drake)*

Recorded at Far Leys by Rodney Drake, date unknown. This delicate piano ballad from Molly Drake is very much in the style of Noël Coward, and takes the viewpoint of a woman whose life hasn't turned out quite as she expected. Although stylistically very different to any of Nick's music, one can easily hear that Molly's vocal approach had a definite influence on her son's vocal phrasing.

## WINTER IS GONE

*(Traditional arr. Nick Drake)*

Recorded at Far Leys. An Appalachian folk song that Nick is thought to have learnt from John Renbourn's eponymous 1965 album; very bluesy, and performed very much in Renbourn's style. Renbourn and Bert Jansch (both big influences on Nick's guitar playing) went on to form the group Pentangle in 1968; Danny Thompson, Pentangle's double-bass player, would later record with both Nick and John Martyn.

## ALL MY TRIALS

*(Traditional)*

Recorded at Far Leys by Rodney Drake, date unknown. Nick and Gabrielle Drake duet on this old Negro spiritual, which was popular during the 'protest' era of the early Sixties and recorded by Peter, Paul & Mary (among others). The Drake siblings' version is utterly charming, their harmonies blending so well that one hopes there are more tapes of them duetting buried somewhere in the vaults.

## KEGELSTAT TRIO

*(W.A. Mozart)*

Recorded at Far Leys by Rodney Drake, date unknown. Nick plays clarinet on this short Mozart piece, accompanied by his aunt (Nancy McDowall) and uncle (Chris McDowall) on viola and piano respectively.

## STROLLING DOWN THE HIGHWAY

*(Bert Jansch)*

Recorded in Aix en Provence. More bluesy folk, and very likeable. It's striking just how extraordinarily accomplished a guitar player Nick was, even at this early stage. He also recorded a version of Jansch's 'Courting Blues', which remains unreleased. Both songs originated from Jansch's debut album.

## PADDLING IN RUSHMERE

*(Traditional)*

Recorded at Far Leys by Rodney Drake, date unknown. An incredibly brief snippet of a piano piece that ends with Nick dissolving in giggles – making it sound as if he was very young indeed when this was recorded.

## COCAINE BLUES

*(Traditional)*

Recorded in Aix en Provence. Based on a blues by Luke Jordan, although Nick is thought to have learnt the song in Aix, either from Dave Van Ronk's album *Folk Singer* or else from Robin Frederick. Van Ronk was a contemporary of Bob Dylan and an important figure in the early Sixties Greenwich Village folk scene; Dylan appropriated Van Ronk's arrangement of 'House Of The Rising Sun' for his first LP, much to the latter's annoyance. An extremely good guitarist influenced by country blues, Van Ronk recorded at least nine albums between the late Fifties and the late Seventies, and died in 2002. Nick's version features some dazzlingly good blues guitar, and the Englishness of his voice isn't as incongruous with the material as you might think – though he does naively mispronounce the word 'cocaine', which is rather endearing (the drug was massively out of favour at the time, and would not become popular again until the late Seventies).

## BLOSSOM

*(Nick Drake)*

Recorded at Far Leys. A folksy farewell to a lost love, stated as an allegory of the seasons and rich in nature imagery. Again, it's reminiscent of early Joni Mitchell, pleasant but unremarkable compared to Nick's later work. His vocals here are husky and waver frequently; possibly he was still unconfident about performing his own material. The song is sometimes also referred to as 'Blossom Friend'.

## BEEN SMOKIN' TOO LONG

*(Robin Frederick)*

Recorded at Far Leys. Another version of Robin Frederick's marijuana blues. See *Time Of No Reply*.

## BLACK MOUNTAIN BLUES

*(Traditional)*

Recorded at Far Leys. A classic 12-bar blues recorded by Bessie Smith, among others. Nick is thought to have learnt the song from Dave Van Ronk's album *Dave Van Ronk Sings Ballads, Blues & A Spiritual*. Good guitar here, but Nick's vocals are somewhat self-conscious and mannered.

## TOMORROW IS A LONG TIME

*(Bob Dylan)*

Recorded in Aix en Provence. Dylan wrote this love song in 1962 for his then girlfriend, Suze Rotolo. He never recorded a studio version of the song, but a live version recorded in New York in 1963 was bootlegged (and finally officially released in 1971 on the *More Bob Dylan Greatest Hits* album). The song was covered by Elvis Presley (in 1966) and Rod Stewart (in 1972), but Nick may well have simply learnt the song from another folk singer in Aix. His version is painfully slow, and he seems to be trying to reinvent the song as English folk. It doesn't work, and wouldn't have done even if he hadn't forgotten one of the lines. Nick also recorded a cover of Dylan's 'Don't Think Twice, It's Alright', which remains unreleased.

## IF YOU LEAVE ME

*(Dave Van Ronk)*

Recorded at Far Leys. Despite Van Ronk's claim to authorship, this is actually a traditional blues; also included on the album *Dave Van Ronk Sings Ballads, Blues & A Spiritual*. Utterly gorgeous, on every level.

## HERE COME THE BLUES

*(Jackson C. Frank)*

Recorded in Aix en Provence. A faithful version, but the song is slight and sounds very much a product of its era. Jackson C. Frank was an American singer-songwriter who was a regular on the London folk-club circuit in the mid-Sixties, and a sometime boyfriend of Sandy Denny. He was enormously influential at the time, and Nick was evidently a devotee, since he recorded covers of three of his songs, all taken from Frank's eponymous 1965 debut album (also known as *Blues Run The Game*), which featured Al Stewart on second guitar and was produced by Paul Simon. Frank began work on a follow-up album in 1968 but never completed it; from then on he spiralled into depression and mental illness, and his tale is an even sadder one than Nick's. He died of pneumonia in 1999, aged 56.

## SKETCH I

*(Nick Drake)*

Recorded at Far Leys. An extremely brief but exquisite guitar instrumental.

## BLUES RUN THE GAME

*(Jackson C. Frank)*

Recorded at Far Leys. This autobiographical slice of folk-blues was the title track of Frank's album, and supposedly the first song he ever wrote. Nick turns in a faithful and appealing performance. Also covered by Simon & Garfunkel, although their version remained unreleased until 1997.

## MY BABY SO SWEET

*(Traditional)*

Recorded at Far Leys. Previously recorded by Dave Van Ronk and also as 'Woman, You're So Sweet' by Blind Boy Fuller. Nick's performance here is unconvincing, as if he's copying a style but his heart isn't truly in it.

## MILK AND HONEY

*(Jackson C. Frank)*

Recorded in Aix en Provence. This also sounds very rooted in its era, and generally not very remarkable. However, Robin Frederick thinks that it was an influence on two of Nick's own songs, 'Day Is Done' and 'Man In A Shed', and you can kind of hear what she means.

## KIMBIE

*(Traditional)*

Recorded in Aix en Provence. So-so folk with Nick in a very Dylanish mode; even so, rather likeable.

## BIRD FLEW BY

*(Nick Drake)*

Recorded at Far Leys. A gentle ballad crowded with nature imagery, its tone almost existential – or else indicating the need for a spiritual side to life. It's also truly excellent, and could have easily fitted in on *Five Leaves Left*. Also known as 'Strange Meeting I'.

## RAIN

*(Nick Drake)*

Recorded at Far Leys. Another farewell to a lost love that employs nature imagery, also known as 'My Love Left With The Rain'. Nick seems very unsure of himself vocally here, and the song itself is very slight. Dropped from inclusion on *Five Leaves Left* early on.

## STRANGE MEETING II

*(Nick Drake)*

Recorded in Aix en Provence, and thus another of Nick's very first attempts at songwriting, which he apparently referred to as "my surrealist song. A sort of funny dream". Robin Frederick thinks it may have been influenced by Alan Resnais' 1961 film fantasy *Last Year In Marienbad*, which was shown in Aix while she and Nick were staying there. See also *Time Of No Reply*.

## DAY IS DONE

*(Nick Drake)*

Demo version recorded by Robert Kirby in Cambridge, with Nick playing Kirby's "rather knocked-about, nylon-strung Spanish guitar", and making the odd mistake en route. Slightly faster than the studio version, but Nick sounds totally assured here, and his performance is strong enough that one hardly misses the string arrangement.

## COME IN TO THE GARDEN

*(Nick Drake)*

Recorded at Far Leys. A different take of the opening song with lots of echo. The song itself is pretty dull.

## WAY TO BLUE

*(Nick Drake)*

Demo recorded by Robert Kirby in Cambridge, with Nick playing Kirby's upright piano (which is somewhat out of tune). This lacks the instrumental break of the studio version and is obviously a lot less epic. On the plus side, it's a much more intimate performance, and even on a slightly clunky piano Nick sounds light years ahead of most of his contemporaries.

## DO YOU EVER REMEMBER?

*(Molly Drake)*

Recorded at Far Leys by Rodney Drake. Another piano ballad from Molly Drake, this time a very brief and poignant one about a lost love, and the effects of time as both a thief and a healer.

# Compilation Albums

**FRUIT TREE**

*Island NDSP 100 (LP); released March 1979.*

Boxed set which contained Nick's three studio albums, with the 'final' four songs ('Rider On The Wheel', 'Hanging On A Star', 'Voice From The Mountain' and 'Black Eyed Dog') tacked onto the end of *Pink Moon*. The set also contained a booklet with text by Arthur Lubow.

**FRUIT TREE**

*Hannibal HNBX 5302 (LP); HNCD 5402 (CD); released August 1986.*

Joe Boyd's reissue of the boxed set again contained the first three studio albums (with *Pink Moon* restored to its original form), plus *Time Of No Reply*. There was also a new booklet, which included Lubow's text (minus a reference to heroin included in the original).

A revised version of *Fruit Tree* was reissued by Island in late 2007. This time the set contained Nick's original three studio albums, plus a DVD of the TV documentary *A Skin Too Few* and a new booklet. We were unable to obtain a copy of this edition in time for a proper review here.

## HEAVEN IN A WILD FLOWER

*Island ILPS 9826 (LP); IMCD 91 (CD); released May 1985.*

Tracks: 'Fruit Tree'/'Cello Song'/'Thoughts Of Mary Jane'/'Northern Sky'/'River Man'/'At The Chime Of A City Clock'/'Introduction'/'Hazey Jane I'/'Hazey Jane II'/'Pink Moon'/'Road'/'Which Will'/'Things Behind The Sun'/'Time Has Told Me'

A good selection compiled by Trevor Dann, but marred by poor sound quality (it was cut from copy tapes rather than the original masters). The title is a quote from one of Nick's favourite poems, William Blake's 'Auguries Of Innocence'. Paul Du Noyer's *NME* review of this compilation referred to Nick as a "genuine genius", and the album sold 20,000 copies on its release.

## WAY TO BLUE: AN INTRODUCTION TO NICK DRAKE

*Island IMCD 196 (CD); released May 1994.*

Tracks: 'Cello Song'/'Hazey Jane I'/'Way To Blue'/'Things Behind The Sun'/'River Man'/'Poor Boy'/'Time Of No Reply'/'From The Morning'/'One Of These Things First'/'Northern Sky'/'Which Will'/'Hazey Jane II'/'Time Has Told Me'/'Pink Moon'/'Black Eyed Dog'/'Fruit Tree'

Compiled and overseen by Joe Boyd (who had been unhappy with the sound quality of the *Heaven In A Wild Flower* collection), and arguably a better selection of material than its predecessor. The album cover photograph by Julian Lloyd shows Nick in a forest, wearing a multicoloured blanket; the album design obscures the fact that Nick is extending a hand towards the viewer, holding a palm full of magic mushrooms.

## A TREASURY

*Island CID 8149 (CD); released 2004.*

Tracks: 'Introduction'/'Hazey Jane II'/'River Man'/'Cello Song'/'Hazey Jane I'/'Pink Moon'/'Poor Boy'/'Magic'/ 'Place To Be'/'Northern Sky'/'Road'/'Fruit Tree'/'Black Eyed Dog'/'Way To Blue'/'From The Morning'/'Plaisir d'Amour' (bonus track)

A near-duplication of *Way To Blue*. The real point of interest here is the 'hidden' track at the end of the album: a 46-second snippet of Nick playing 'Plaisir d'Amour', an 18th-century French tune than had been popularised in the Sixties by Joan Baez (among others). Doubtless intended as a nice bonus, its inclusion was seen by fans who already owned everything else here as nothing less than a blatant rip-off. It's strange, since this situation could have easily been avoided by including the track on *Made To Love Magic* or *Family Tree* instead.

# Oddities, Rarities & Covers

## FEATURING NICK DRAKE

### MICK AUDSLEY/*DEEP THE DARK* AND *DEVILLED WATERS*

Nick plays uncredited guitar on these two albums (both on Sonet) by bluegrass player Audsley. Both albums were produced by Robert Kirby.

### *INTERPLAY*

A double album produced as a teaching aid by the educational publisher Longmans, recorded in 1970 or 1971 and released in 1972. Nick plays bass guitar on 'I Wish I Was A Single Girl Again' (with Vivien Fowler on vocals), and guitar on two other tracks: 'Full Fathom Five' and 'With My Swag All On My Shoulder (with Robert Kirby on vocals).

# FEATURING OTHER ARTISTS

## THE WARLOCK MUSIC ACETATE

In June 1970 Joe Boyd decided to commission a special recording of various songs by Warlock songwriters John and Beverley Martyn, Ed Carter, Mike Heron and Nick Drake, the aim being to stimulate interest in their work and persuade record labels and other musicians to consider recording cover versions of their material. Taking part in the session at Sound Techniques studios were Jim Capaldi of Traffic on drums, Fotheringay's Pat Donaldson on bass and Fairport's Simon Nicol on guitar, plus two session singers: Linda Peters (then Boyd's girlfriend, later Linda Thompson) and Elton John (who at this point had just released his second album). One hundred acetate copies of these recordings were pressed, though very few genuine copies still exist (perhaps as few as seven). In 2004, a genuine copy fetched £3,000 on eBay.

Elton John sings the four Drake songs included on the acetate: 'Day Is Done', 'Saturday Sun', 'Way To Blue' and 'Time Has Told Me'. These are all performed in a fairly rocky style – 'Day Is Done' being the standout track – and sound very much as you'd expect if you're familiar with Elton's first two studio albums. When he took part in the session Elton was already a fan of *Five Leaves Left*, and is on record enthusing over the "beautiful, haunting quality" of Nick's songs. He later told Trevor Dann that the Drake songs "suited me; they sound like they were written on the piano". These four tracks are widely available on bootlegs, although some pressings substitute Elton's version of Beverley Martyn's 'Sweet Honesty' for the credited 'Saturday Sun'.

## THE NEW YORK TRIBUTE GIG

In November 1977 a concert celebrating Nick Drake's music was held in St Ann's Church in Brooklyn, and was also broadcast by WFUV-FM radio (so tapes may well exist somewhere). Some 21 of Nick's songs were performed by various English and American artists, including Peter Holsapple, Peter Blegvad, Terre Roche and Syd Straw.

## THE BARBICAN TRIBUTE GIG

Organised by Kate St John of The Dream Academy (who had dedicated their hit 'Life In A Northern Town' to Nick), this tribute concert featured versions of Nick's songs performed by Robyn Hitchcock, Beth Orton, Bernard Butler, David Gray, Jackie Dankworth, Robin Frederick and Beverley Martyn. Not known to have been recorded, but we live in hope.

## SCOTT APPEL/*NINE OF SWORDS*

*Kicking Mule Records, number unknown; released in 1989; reissued as Schoolkids Records SKR 1521 in 1995.*

At some point in 1987 Rodney and Molly Drake gave American guitarist Appel their blessing to record his versions of unreleased songs from Nick's 'work tape'. Alongside Appel's own compositions (plus covers of the traditional 'Spencer The Rover' and Phil Colclough's 'Song For Ireland'), this album includes versions of Nick's 'Bird Flew By', 'Blossom' and 'Rain' (incorrectly titled 'Our Season' here), plus covers of 'Place To Be' and 'Parasite'. (See *Family Tree* for reviews of the unreleased songs.) There's also an unfinished guitar fragment of Nick's that Appel had developed (both receive composer credit), titled 'Far Leys', which is utterly delightful – more folk than blues, and decidedly joyous. Appel performs with a full band (including synthesised strings), his own vocals and guitar frequently double-tracked. Appel's vocal style places him squarely in the tradition of American folk singers such as Tom Rush and Tom Paxton, but his guitar playing on Nick's songs is uncannily like the original – Molly Drake thought that it sounded so much like Nick that "it makes my heart turn over". For nearly 20 years (prior to the release of *Family Tree* in 2007), *Nine Of Swords* was the only legitimate way of hearing these unreleased songs; sadly, the album is currently out of print, and copies now fetch £75 or more. A reissue was due in 2000, but didn't happen; hopefully someone will soon remedy the situation.

## SCOTT APPEL/*PARHELION*

*One Hand Clapping Records OMC 0015; released 1998.*

Appel's follow-up to *Nine Of Swords* continued in the same vein, and apart from Appel's original material (and covers of songs by Steve Miller, Fairport Convention and Moby Grape) also included versions of Nick's 'Road' (an outtake from *Swords*), 'Hazey Jane I' and 'From The Morning' (both from the *Brittle Days* covers album) and a collection of three of Nick's unfinished instrumental fragments Appel had completed under the umbrella title of 'Brittle Days' (and again credited to Drake and Appel; the third section of this had originally been played by Nick on piano, but is played on guitar here). It's a meandering work rather than a memorable one, but has moments of great beauty. Scott Appel died in March 2003, aged 48.

## VARIOUS ARTISTS/*BRITTLE DAYS: A TRIBUTE TO NICK DRAKE*

*Imaginary Records ILLCD 026; released 1995.*

'River Man' (The Changelings)/'At The Chime Of A City Clock' (The High Llamas)/'Pink Moon' (Loop)/'Road' (No Man)/'Cello Song' (The Walkabouts)/'Joey' (Shelleyann Orphan)/'From The Morning' (Scott Appel)/'Fruit Tree' (The Times)/'Know' (Martyn Bates)/'Voice From The Mountain' (The Swinging Swine)/'Time Has Told Me' (Nikki Sudden & The French Revolution)/'Fly' (Tracy Santa)/'Northern Sky' (Clive Gregson)/'Hazey Jane' (Scott Appel)/'River Man' (R. Stevie Moore)

This collection of Drake cover versions has been deleted for years, but is well worth tracking down for a few of its tracks, notably The Swinging Swine's gorgeous, instrumentally lush 'Voice From The Mountain', Tracy Santa's stately, countryish take on 'Fly' and Clive Gregson's heartfelt reading of 'Northern Sky'. Both of Scott Appel's two tracks are also excellent, but these were subsequently released on *Parhelion*, along with 'Brittle Days', which had also been contributed to this project but was (strangely) not included. The Changelings' Indian-style arrangement of 'River Man' is also mildly interesting, but everything else here lies somewhere between unremarkable and irritating.

For many years there's been talk of organising an all-star Nick Drake tribute album along these lines, featuring some of the high-profile acts known to like his music, but so far there's still no sign of it getting off the ground.

**Also available, but not located in time for inclusion in this book:**

Keith James/*The Songs Of Nick Drake* (James regularly tours Britain with his Nick Drake tribute performance); Tony Reif/*Poor Boy* (containing jazz versions of Nick's songs); *Jeremy Flies: A Tribute To Nick Drake* (a compilation of cover versions by contemporary Australian artists); *Gilbert Ibsen Plays Nick Drake* (cover versions by the Belgian guitarist); *Time Has Told Me: A Nick Drake Tribute* (cover versions by classical pianist Christopher O'Riley); Nick Smart/*Black Eyed Dog* (more jazz interpretations).

# Unreleased Works

## UNRELEASED SONGS

The following songs by Nick Drake remain unreleased, although not all of them may have actually been recorded.

### BLUE SEASON

Unfinished. Supposedly a very despondent song about isolation and failure.

### BRITTLE DAYS

An instrumental sketch recorded at Far Leys that Scott Appel later completed (on his *Parhelion* album).

### FAR LEYS

Another instrumental sketch later completed by Scott Appel (on his *Nine Of Swords* album).

### GO YOUR WAY AND I'LL JUST FOLLOW

A song that Nick is known to have played live during 1969. No other details known.

## JOEY IN MIND

Another song about 'Joey' (possibly Jo D'Arcy, an Aix girl-friend). The lyrics seem to indicate that Nick genuinely loved her, and that much of his nostalgia for Aix is due to his missing her. The lyric also namechecks "Mary Jane", and given the Aix context would seem to imply that the name is meant to represent Robin Frederick.

## MICKEY'S TUNE

Supposedly a song about a bolder, more outgoing friend.

## OUTSIDE

An unfinished song about withdrawing from the world and returning to the safety of home.

## RECKLESS JANE

Beverley Martyn claims to have co-written this song with Nick, but it was probably never finished and may not have even been recorded.

In addition to the material released in 2007 on *Family Tree*, there also remain at least four other cover versions recorded by Nick (at Far Leys and/or Aix) in the vaults:

## COURTING BLUES

*(Bert Jansch)*

The original version of this folksy love song comes from Jansch's eponymous 1965 debut album.

## GET TOGETHER

*(Dino Valenti)*

Dino Valenti (a.k.a. Chet Powers) should have been a founder member of San Francisco's Quicksilver Messenger Service when they formed in 1966, but was in jail on a drugs charge at the time and didn't join the band until 1970. This song was first recorded by the We Five and Hamilton Camp in 1965, by Jefferson Airplane in 1966 and by The Youngbloods (who had a hit with it) in 1967. Practically a hippie anthem, the song was also covered in concert by numerous artists of the era (I saw Joni Mitchell perform it live in 1969). Also recorded by the Indigo Girls in the Eighties.

## DON'T THINK TWICE, IT'S ALL RIGHT

*(Bob Dylan)*

Supposedly a fairly fast version of the bittersweet love song from *The Freewheelin' Bob Dylan*.

## SUMMERTIME

*(George Gershwin / Du Bose Heyward)*

The timeless standard that originated in the 1935 musical *Porgy & Bess*. Nick may well have heard the version recorded by The Zombies on their 1965 debut album (and Nick's voice is remarkably similar at times to that of Zombies vocalist Colin Blunstone); when Nick recorded his version is unknown, but it's also just possible that he might have been influenced by the version by Janis Joplin (with Big Brother & The Holding Company, from their 1968 album *Cheap Thrills*). Regardless, the song's nature imagery would have certainly appealed to him, and would have fitted well alongside the songs he was writing himself.

# THE SOURCE TAPES

## THE AIX TAPE

According to Robin Frederick, this tape was recorded in Aix en Provence in April or May 1967 by Nick's friend James, using an early Philips cassette recorder. It's a 35-minute tape of Nick playing a selection of cover versions and his own very early material, with comments by Nick on each song. The tape surfaced in the Nineties and was acquired by the Drake Estate. Eight tracks appeared on *Family Tree*.

## THE TANWORTH 'WORK' TAPE

There is almost certainly more than one tape recorded at Far Leys featuring Nick, but reference has been made to a 'work' tape that is four hours long and contains both cover versions and Nick's own early material. There may well be much duplication of material with the Aix tape, as well as demo versions of songs that would later be recorded for the first two Island albums. Fourteen tracks from these tapes appeared on *Family Tree*.

## THE KIRBY TAPES

Robert Kirby recorded tapes of Nick playing his early songs in Kirby's room in Cambridge over a number of weeks during spring 1968. Nick played guitar, and also Kirby's piano on 'Way To Blue', 'Made To Love Magic' and 'Saturday Sun'. There are thought to have been about 30-minutes worth of recordings, but some of the tapes may not have survived. Two tracks appeared on *Made To Love Magic*, another two on *Family Tree*.

# THE BATEMAN ROOM
# CONCERT

Recorded just before Easter 1968. The concert included 'Time Of No Reply', 'I Was Made To Love Magic', 'The Thoughts Of Mary Jane', 'Day Is Done', 'My Love Left With The Rain'. As previously mentioned, with no rehearsal beforehand of Kirby's string arrangements the results were somewhat shambolic ("crap" according to Kirby). Recording engineer Peter Rice subsequently recorded Nick playing several other songs (solo) in a friend's room at Cambridge, and added these to the five Bateman songs for Nick to use as a demo tape. Nothing from this tape has yet surfaced.

# UNTITLED MUSICAL

Nick plays guitar on the demo tape of an unfinished Robert Kirby project – a musical inspired by medieval mystery plays. Music by Kirby, lyricist unknown. Probably recorded in 1971. A tape of this may still exist somewhere in Kirby's archives.

# RADIO 1 SESSION

Recorded and broadcast by John Peel in August 1969. Contains unaccompanied solo versions of 'Time Of No Reply', 'Cello Song', 'River Man' and 'Three Hours'. Peel confirmed in 2001 that the original tape had been destroyed (which was BBC policy at the time); an incomplete version has been bootlegged. When Peel asks Nick what he's been doing recently, Nick replies, "Wasting my time in Cambridge".

# SECOND JOHN PEEL SESSION

Details unknown. The session was never broadcast (if it ever actually took place at all), and the tape is again believed to have been destroyed.

# NIGHT RIDE SESSION

Broadcast in April 1970. Again, the tape for this Radio 2 broadcast is believed to have been destroyed. Iain Cameron, who played on the session, has stated that somewhere between four and eight songs were recorded, including a version of 'Saturday Sun' on which Nick played celeste.

# THE WOOD TAPE

Nick's parents believed that he made some recordings at John Wood's home studio sometime during 1974. Since Nick was in pretty bad shape at the time, if this tape even exists it may well prove to be a disappointment.

# THE CREED TAPE

Jason Creed, editor of the fanzine *Pink Moon*, is in possession of a tape featuring unreleased versions of 'Place To Be', 'Hazey Jane I', 'Time Has Told Me' and 'Black Eyed Dog'. The sources of these recordings are unknown.

# ISLAND OUT-TAKES

More out-takes from the first two Island albums may well exist, but it seems probable that the cream of the crop has already been released.

# Index